Circus in a Suitcase

by Reg Bolton
illustrated by Jo Hignett

NEW PLAYS INCORPORATED
Box 371
Bethel, CT 06801

CIRCUS IN A SUITCASE

WHAT IS A CIRCUS?

Whenever somebody does something amazing, in front of an audience — something which seems incredible, and superhuman, you have the elements of Circus.

In the earliest records of all civilizations, from Egypt to England, from China to Rome, there are stories and pictures showing performers doing what we recognize as Circus acts. Juggling eggs, balancing on a rope, somersaulting over knives, swallowing swords, eating fire, training animals to dance — all these things have been done for hundreds, even thousands, of years, and we, the audience, are still amazed.

The Circus Maximus in Rome held 300,000 spectators, two thousand years ago, sitting and standing in a massive oval amphitheatre, watching feats of speed, skill, and spectacle — but also scenes of cruelty and horror. From the Roman Circus, we have inherited little but the name.

In 1778, in London, Charles Dibdin first gave the name "Circus" to the new style of entertainment made popular by Philip Astley. Sergeant-Major Astley, a riding master, erected a 42-foot diameter ring, and was the first man to combine horsemanship and comedy, and to fill the bill with street performers — ropewalkers, jugglers, tumblers, dancing bears, puppets and fireworks.

In the 1940's in the U.S.A., the Ringling Brothers, Barnum and Bailey Circus used 109 railway carriages to carry up to 1,400 people, hundreds of animals, and their enormous 4-ring Big Top, which seated over 10,000 paying customers. In the Soviet Union, there are 62 permanent circus buildings, and one of the finest circus schools in the world, in Moscow. In San Francisco, the Pickle Family Circus, starting as a community-based street theatre company, now tours world-wide with a show of clowning and human skills, as does the Australian Circus Oz. These troupes perform, not in the traditional Big Top, but in theatres and TV studios.

Today the age of the large-scale tenting circus is over. I love the Circus, and I'm witnessing the traditional tenting companies dwindling and deteriorating. In England, the dozen or so touring circuses are struggling to stay afloat in the face of apathetic audiences, restrictive taxes, and ever-increasing rules and regulations imposed by local licensing authorities. Some I have seen in the last few years have been excellent in every way — but, alas, only half full. It hardly seems possible that the proprietors can keep up the energy and standards which have entranced millions of spectators over the past 200 years.

But I'm not despondent. On the contrary, I'm inspired and full of hope for the future of the Circus.

You see, what has happened is that the huge 3- and 4-ring circuses have made the magic of the performers' skills so remote as to be almost puppet-like and the televised, edited, sugar-coated circus spectacular has totally warped the expectations of the audience. Now, when a family goes to a visiting circus in the park, and sees a trapeze flier perform only one or two somersaults, they are disappointed! At home on the TV they saw, close-up, in vivid color, with slow-motion action, replays of the Circus World Championships, the ultimate *triple* somersault. Now they'll be satisfied with nothing less.

On TV, one amazing act follows another, with no break except a glossy commercial, or sweet-talking intros from a popular D.J. dressed as a Ringmaster. In the Big Top in the park, they have to wait while tackle is checked and cages are dismounted. The Ringmaster is a stranger to them, the music is less than perfect, the animals smell and the seats are hard.

TV has spoiled the audience.

The same goes for clowning. Joey Grimaldi, king of clowns, performed in theatres where he was never more than 50 feet from his audience, and all London swarmed to see him, for 30 years. He could draw a laugh by wiggling his ears. Astley's Circus ring was only 42 feet across. As the tent got bigger and bigger, clowns became distant, colorful, pause fillers. They had to rely on burning houses and exploding cars to make any impact on a vast audience. The greatest clowns of all — Chaplin, Keaton, Laurel and Hardy — had to find a new medium, the movies, where the audience could see them close up, and in comfort.

So, why am I inspired and hopeful for the future?

Because Circus is coming back to where it started. To the streets.

In the "private sector" more and more young people are learning skills and taking to the streets to busk for a living. Our English towns on market days are gradually taking on the excitement and variety portrayed by Hogarth's 18th century engravings of Southwark Fair, with jugglers, magicians, musicians and tightrope walkers.

The "public-sector," those travelling or resident mountebanks who have entertained "at-court," since the time of Pharoahs, to amuse the overprivileged and bored folk of the court and make banquets go with a swing, have today become patronized, not by the royal family or local barons, but by Arts Councils and local authorities. We play, not for the aristocracy, but for the population at large — in schools, theatres, parks and housing estates.

The effect is like magic. While people will be unimpressed by a mid-air double somersault in a Big Top, they will be amazed by a back-flip on their own doorstep! A circus band can be brilliantly dressed, and play like Gods, but how can they hope to compete with little Jimmy and his friends next door, out in the back yard playing a fanfare on drum, trumpet, and violin!

On the streets of Paris, London, New York, Peking — maybe every city in the world — jugglers, fire-eaters, contortionists, snake-charmers and escapologists are attracting a circle of on-lookers, performing "superhuman" feats, and creating a one-man Circus. And in towns of the U.S.A. and Britain, groups of children, like those I'll describe in Pilton, Scotland, have formed neighborhood circuses. They have brought the streets to life, and given the children and their families a whole new dimension to their lives.

Now, you can do it!

If you can attract and arrange an audience, if you can amuse, entertain and AMAZE them, you have a Circus. Read this book, gather some friends together, learn the techniques, collect some props and costumes, and begin to rehearse your own CIRCUS IN A SUITCASE.

THE PILTON CIRCUS

"I'm Michael," he said,

"Oh, yes . . . ?"

"I can juggle."

He was just sixteen. Small, skinny, but not shy. He had heard that I was looking for school-drop-outs to join a job-creation project in Edinburgh. Jobs were scarce, and for a 16-year-old, leaving school with no qualifications whatsoever, living in Pilton, with 20% adult unemployment, his prospects were nil. Some of his friends were lucky. One was a milk roundsman, one was an apprentice, one or two had places on this newly invented "Job Creation Project."

"I hear you're starting a circus," he said.

"Not exactly," I said,

I explained that as Arts Coordinator my job was to advise and run creative activities in Craigmillar. Mike knew Craigmillar as a huge housing project on the other side of the city. I worked for the Craigmillar Festival Society, supervising a "Job Creation Program" where twenty youngsters of 16 and 17 would learn skills and use them for community service.

Some would form a band, some would become an audio/visual team, some would help produce the local newspaper. My particular interest was the group of eight youngsters who would become the community theatre team. I would be training the theatre group by teaching some of my own skills — juggling . . . unicycling . . . stilt walking. But, actually . . .

"So you are starting a circus?"

"Yes . . . I suppose I am."

"Can I work for you? That's what I want to do."

Making a Performer of Mike

As a theatre trainee, Mike was a dead loss. His accent was as strong and Scottish as Edinburgh Castle Rock. He could never remember lines and, what was most aggravating to his director, his face would split in a vacant and uncontrollable grin whenever he *did* do something right, or whenever he was amused by another actor, or whenever he saw a friend in the audience, or, quite often, for no reason at all.

So — he was a rotten actor. But he could juggle — and that's what he wanted to do. At the end of the day, he'd still be there, juggling his 3 apples to a pulp, or falling off my unicycle time and time again until, one memorable day, he actually rode the thing right across the room. That day he grinned all the way home, a strange sight to commuting bus-passengers.

Two weeks later, it was their turn to grin. Alongside the bus at the red light was Mike — on the unicycle — riding home.

4

There's nothing in the ancient austere law books of Scotland to deal with a 16-year-old riding a one-wheeled vehicle along Princes Street.

P. C. McDonald: "You shouldn't be riding that on the road, laddie. Get on the pavement."

P. C. McBride: "Get that cycle off the pavement, laddie. It's a danger to pedestrians."

So Michael became very adept at leaping off the uni, and tucking it under his arm at the sight of a blue uniform.

Back home, on the streets of Pilton, he wasn't bothered by the police. They had other things to do. So each evening, Mike and his brothers and friends would spend hours riding this one unicycle up and down the road, round and round the lampposts, on grass, concrete, and asphalt, forwards and backwards, fast and slow, alone, or carrying a wee kiddie on their shoulders.

This could have been the end of the story (it was virtually the end of my poor unicycle). But Mike had other ideas. At the Edinburgh Festival he had seen, and met, the American clown Bob Berky. He was impressed by Berky's skills, his style, his ability to charm an Edinburgh audience ... and by the fact that he was earning a living! Mike decided he would do a solo clown show.

He borrowed a costume from Craigmillar, make-up and unicycle from me, and brought his own juggling balls. His first show was in a wooden hut, at the local adventure playground, to an audience of sixty local children. When they acutally laughed at his jokes, applauded his skills, and shouted "MORE!" at the end, his fate was sealed.

A Circus in Pilton?

It's difficult for me to describe Pilton, because it is *home* to so many of my friends. But even the people who live there will admit that the amenities are substandard. The blocks and blocks of houses seem never ending, relieved only by treeless, windswept grass areas. Certainly, there are no architects or town planners among the 16,000 residents. There's no cinema, swimming pool, no sports center, and very few shops, pubs and playgrounds. Many of the tenement blocks are empty with windows boarded up, and gardens littered with glass and rubbish. Interspersed with the desolation are well-kept patches of flowers and shrubs. But this is the backdrop — wrecked cars, dogs upsetting trashcans, playgrounds glittering with broken glass. These things are resented, but accepted as normal. This is Pilton, and this is where Michael started a circus.

The club had started on Tuesday evenings in the small playhut ... anything but ideal facilities for what he was trying to do. But the club caught the imagination of a wide age range, and soon had so many people coming that there was no room to work in. This was a happy problem — one that could be sorted by splitting the club into attendance on two separate nights.

Then, disaster. The playhut was broken into four times in succession, and the last time set on fire. No premises, and the little equipment they had, lost. This was a time when they lost quite a number of interested young people. It was winter, and they had nowhere to meet indoors.

They did retain a nucleus of very good young people who tried hard to make the playhut useable, but the building was delcared unsafe. Eventually they were offered the Y.W.C.A. Triangle Club Hall on a temporary basis. This was ideal, but they were severely restricted for lack of equipment. Also, Michael had to look to his own career, and he was offered a job with a professional circus.

It was at this point that Michael met me. I started to come along to the club, and brought my equipment. The club sprang to life again. We were asked to take part in the Pilton Festival.

The First Show

Let me recall that Halloween, 1979. Some would say that the club wasn't ready for it, and there's some truth in that. Very few of the 25 kids involved had performed before. The club had none of their own equipment, and hardly any costumes; they hadn't rehearsed with music. But they knew and remember three things: keep quiet in the corridor; do their act as rehearsed; and come back for the final parade.

The dressing room was bedlam. The "lads" —Mike, his brother, Alan, Dougie, Ray and Pete —all about 15 to 17 years old — were putting on fancy costumes for the first time in their lives. As if this weren't enough degradation, they found I expected them to wear make-up!! Ugh! Eventually they settled for a uniform of white face, and debonnaire black moustaches.

From that day to this, they always perform in this same make-up. What they discovered in that first show is that make-up, far from making you conspicuous, enables you to hide yourself behind a mask, and if you're all the same, you're simply a member of the troupe.

The girls disappeared to somewhere private to get their leotards on, but in the main, that small room was full of bodies of all shapes and sizes —boys, girls, children, adults, fat ones, thin ones, quiet ones and boisterous ones. A total mixture of types, but all working together to the same aim.

In the hall, the capacity crowd has listened to the Senior Citizens choir, and were now being amused and a little shocked by the local minister doing a comedy routine in drag.

Our gang were "quietly" filing out into the corridor. Willie, on stilts, suddenly panicked because he thought he wouldn't get through the door. Little Pete on his unicycle was terrified in case the floor of the hall might be too slippery. Lizzie and her friends, the other acrobats, were giggling and shivering, and forever tugging their leotards down at the back.

But the most nervous of all was Mike. He was to be ringmaster. He had to remember "lines"; he had to speak clearly; and he had to rely on his brothers and friends to "do it right."

"And believe it or not," the minister was saying in the microphone, "these youngsters have actually trained themselves right here in Pilton. We proudly present the Pilton Children's Circus!"

I pressed the button on the cassette player. "The Entry of the Gladiators" rang out and, as the cymbals clashed, the audience was amazed to see wee Willie, Bob and Acki stride into the hall, eight feet tall, their wooden feet clumping on the floor, and their arms swinging confidently as they took up positions for the dance routine. The music changed; they marched, they waltzed, they boogied, and then, incredibly, they linked arms and performed the can-can.

From the start the audience was with them, clapping enthusiastically along with the music.

They had rehearsed this routine for weeks, and after two minutes it was over. But now came the good bit. This was something they understood. Mike the ringmaster became Mike the referee. He produced a whistle and a ball, and introduced the two soccer teams. Scotland —"Hooray!" and England —"Boo! Hiss!" Soccer on stilts!

I can't remember the result. I remember four members of the audience being used as goal posts. I remember the ball flying dangerously low and very fast over the heads of the audience, and I remember 16-year-old Acki lunging to reach the ball, and going into a fast and graceless split!

One act followed another, more or less without a hitch. Stevie, the chief clown, herded his troupe on to fill each gap with bits of anarchic nonsense. The unicycle act was a great success, as Mike and the boys hurtled up the aisles at break-neck speed, and performed twists and turns in tiny spaces. Big Dougie —aged 17— did his incredible running-mount on the 6' high "giraffee" unicycle, which is like a pole vault with nowhere to put your pole! And finally, two of the lads circled each other, linking hands, while a small clown hung precariously between them.

The acrobats performed rolls, handsprings, walkovers, and cartwheels. But what made their act so much more than the boring old school display were three new elements:
● Drum rolls and cymbal clashes, which pulled applause out of the audience.
● The clown who did it all wrong, but highlighted the skills of the girl acrobats.
● The finale, when the big boys hoisted the small girls effortlessly onto their shoulders for the human pyramid.

I remember Mike's big build-up.
    "You've seen the pyramids of Egypt! You've seen the pyramids of Rome!
    Now, Ladies and Gentlemen, the Pilton Human Pyramid!"
APPLAUSE. Pyramids of Rome??

There were about six acts, including a juggling act which, looking back, was incredibly basic —and they'd be ashamed of it now. But at the time, and in that context, the fact that their children had learned all these skills —in their own time, without the help of schools or parents —and had the confidence to stand out there and *do* it was astonishing to the audience.

As the final parade ended, and the stilt walkers bent down to get through the door, I knew that this group had a future. The circus had come from the streets, and was their own creation.

There would always be a place for me and others to contribute what we could, and individuals within the group would come and go —but the essential Pilton Circus would survive.

Continued Training Sessions

After that fist show, training continued every Tuesday. Mike would start the evening with wild, energetic crazy games, always including unicycle tag. In this game, those who could ride unicycles would chase those who couldn't. Each week more and more joined the chasers.

More terrifying were the standing-on-shoulders relay races, and stilts obstacle courses. Sometimes, if the devil was in them, everything would come together. Unicyclists would dart between stilt-walkers' legs, while jugglers hurled balls and clubs to try to knock them off.

If this sounds most un-club-like behavior, remember that these kids did not normally go to clubs. The circus to them was a perfect blend of sport and danger, and showing off. In fact, there was a strong structure of self-discipline within the group, as any newcomer found to his cost if he spoiled a rehearsal by being noisy or careless at the wrong time.

The bulk of the evening would be in groups —unicycle, stilts, acrobatics and juggling. Those who could taught those who couldn't, and together they developed new crazy ideas.

I lent them a miniature 2-child pantomime horse costume, and within ten minutes, the horse was cantering round the room at ceiling level, standing on the shoulders of two unicyclists!

When the balls were lost, they juggled handkerchiefs, half-bricks, and even traffic cones.

They never elected a formal committee, but the older children, plus two mums and the play-leader, began fund raising by applying to charitable trusts, and holding sponsored events. I was with them for a circus in a car-park which raised 30 pounds, and I read in the newspaper about their 15-mile sponsored unicycle ride to Edinburgh Airport, and numerous yard sales.

Belle and Liz, the mums, worked away at making costumes; the dads made stilts, and by the first spring they were performing two or three shows each month —for old people, children, and local galas.

Tours and a Festival

In July 1 joined a mixed group of 14 kids and four adults on a wonderful tour of the west of Scotland. The route had been arranged to give the kids a break from big-city life, and they found themselves performing on village greens, and fields by running streams, to crowds of astonished local folk and holiday-makers. For the first time, these youngsters were able to travel afield to represent their home town. Back home the name Pilton was synonymous with trouble, but far from home the name came to be associated with the aspiration, enterprise and success of this group.

They took the ferry boat across to the lovely Isle of Arran, and the passengers were more than a little surprised to see young Pele riding round and round the deck, determined to be the first person to unicycle across the Firth of Clyde.

In August, they got together with the Craigmillar Circus Club, and made the mome.. journey over the border to Manchester, England, to the first Community Circus Festival. The reputation went before them, and the English crowd were rightly impressed by their brash, daredevil show, which included the death dive (dive forward roll) over 16 recumbent bodies.

Craigmillar collected the "Golden Balls" juggling award. But Pilton won the bass drum for their human juggling marathon, and Pele and Dougie, who both recorded the same fastest time for the unicycle obstacle course, won the coveted customized unicycle. The only thing they didn't win was the stilts soccer tournament. Typically, they tried too hard, and fell over too many times. At one time, they were all down, and the picker-upper couldn't move fast enough. The local Mancheser-Hulme team just strolled across the battlefield, to score the winning goal of a very popular victory.

A week after this great outing, three of the kids flew (yes, in an airplane) to Manchester again to appear on a nationwide television chat show, on the same bill as the world-famous mime, Marcel Marceau.

Holding it Together

It would be easy to say that since then the Pilton Circus has gone from strength to strength. It hasn't. It has had its ups and downs. Some older members have left. Mike is earning his living as a clown and circus teacher, which has taken him to many parts of Great Britain, to France and to Israel. The Youth Club has closed for repair, and Liz and Belle are finding it difficult to hold everything together. But without a regular meeting place, the Pilton Circus is still there. I went back in mid-February, and sent word around the streets that a new show was wanted. After just one rehearsal, we were ready to go, and the next day arrived at St. Andrews, the very dignified and historic university town. The Pilton Circus was quite unabashed, and treated these famous tree-lined cobbled streets just like their own Pilton streets. The population was surprised, affronted, but completely won over, and the Pilton Circus was declared the hit of the St. Andrews Festival. Once again, the name Pilton came to signify something positive and optimistic.

It's difficult to assess the impact of the Circus on the people of Pilton. Obviously there is a great deal of pride among the families of the individual children concerned. Furthermore, many residents of Pilton are tremendously encouraged to see so much press and television coverage referring to Pilton in a positive way after years of bad publicity. As they travel in Scotland and England (and a tour of France is now being planned) the Circus is a great roving ambassador for Pilton.

In the words of John Thomson, the youth leader at their playground: "The Pilton Circus Club could and should be just the tip of the iceberg of what can be offered to the young people of this area, now and in the future. It shows what can be done to give children and young people in Pilton the chance to gain new experiences and do something exciting and worthwhile with their time."

rcus just grew naturally; it was the right thing in the right place at the right time. In tion, however, you may not have this luxury of time to let things develop. You may have to be ready by a deadline — by the summer holidays, or the end of term. Or, alternatively, you may feel the need for a solid organization *before* you launch your circus — something to impress funding bodies and the press, to reassure parents, and to give *you* more confidence.

This was the case when I founded the Flint Circus in North Wales, where I was starting a new activity in a small town. Flint has a rich cultural heritage, but is now suffering increasing unemployment, especially among the young. The headquarters of the Circus Club was to be either a church or a local youth club. For both the Church Club was to be either a church hall or a local youth club. For both the Church and the Youth and Community Department, I drew up this carefully planned structure in advance, and succeeded in sticking fairly closely to it in the months that followed.

Stage One — The Soft Sell

Heads began to turn when I rode down Flint High Street on a unicycle. I was wearing a suit and tie, and carrying a briefcase, and not apparently trying to raise a laugh, attract attention, or collect money. The desired effect was, of course, to get people talking, and speculating.

Another approach was through the children themselves. I booked a professional clown to perform his show in the primary schools, and when the children were excited and inspired, I let them know that soon they would get the chance to try these things themselves.

Stage Two — The Hard Sell

Careful planning and a wide net were used for the next step — the public meeting. I sent a letter out to all the local media, town councillors, head-teachers, churches, scouts, and other youth and community organizations:

> The Community Circus is a new concept in Flint, but it is one that has been accepted more and more in many different parts of the country. In at least 12 towns in England and Scotland, local people have come together to help their children form real, entertaining, Circus troupes.
>
> The advantages are obvious:
>
> - Adults, teenagers and children can all work together.
> - There's something for everybody to do, from grannies to toddlers.
> - It provides scope for the clever, the quiet, the bold and the noisy.
> - You can work indoors or out.
> - You can achieve quick results.
> - You can really put your neighborhood on the map.
> - It's fun.
>
> A group of local people have decided to form the Flint Children's Circus, to be based at the Boroughgrove Youth Centre. We would very much value your support. You can help in three ways:
>
> - Send people to us — children *or* adults, who you think could help, or who would benefit from joining our group.
> - Support us. Mention us in your press reports, and at meetings. Help us get the necessary funding and facilities.
> - Come and see us. Before long, we'll be on the T.V., and at every local carnival and fete, so you won't be able to avoid seeing us! But for now — please come to our
>
>   FIRST PUBLIC MEETING!
>   Details attached . . .

This letter didn't bring a great number of people to the meeting, but it sowed the seed, and the town now knew what we were attempting, and would wait and see what happened.

The Media came — they always do! There's something about the combination of Circus and local children that is irresistible to newsmen — especially television. So, be warned, and be ready for a press invasion the moment they hear about you.

11

To bring in local adults and children, we used posters in shop windows, inviting the public to an attractive *free show*. The advertised program was:

- A free show by the Chinley Children's Circut, Derbyshire.
- Demonstration of Circus Techniques by Reg Bolton, Director of the Suitcase Circus Project.
- Slide film show of the 1980 National Children's Circus Gala.
- Exhibition of circus equipment, posters and books.
- A Meeting to set up a working committee for the Flint Children's Circus.
- Refreshments.

NOTE: This is a meeting for interested adults. Children are very welcome — if they bring their *parents*.

Stage Three — The First Public Meeting

I had invited the Chinley group, had formed only 6 months earlier, to make the 50-mile journey to Flint, to show us it could be done. It was clear to the audience that these Chinley children were very much like the children of Flint. And yet they were performing impossible feats! They were juggling, unicycling, and stilt-walking, right there in the Flint Youth Club. "If they can do it, so can we!"

I then gave a demonstration of how to strap on stilts, and how to mount a unicycle, with some hilarious help from the audience.

The slide show was full of sun and color, very exhilarating on a January night. It showed hundreds of children taking part in the first grand get-together of community circuses in Manchester. It showed the vivid potential of home-made costumes, the great variety of pantomimed animals — from elephant to crocodile, the laughter, the risks and the enormous fun to be had from Circus, by adult and child alike.

Then came the meeting. I explained the way I foresaw the development in Flint, and answered questions (and asked a few). Finally, I listed the jobs to be done, and asked for volunteers and nominations. We elected a committee who met briefly at the end of the evening, and got down to business the following week. They elected a chairman, shared out areas of responsibility, and, after a week or two, invited the children onto the committee to represent the views of the young members. They decided:

- The club would meet once a week. Children would pay 10 p. for each class. The first hour would be open to everybody. The second hour would be restricted to a smaller, advanced group at no extra cost.
- Extra rehearsals would be called when necessary.
- The committee would decide which engagements to accept.
- The Director would have the right to decide which children would perform in each show.

ORGANIZATIONAL STRUCTURE

Whether you decide on an informal or formal structure is up to you. I suggest the following responsibilities should be covered by your group. You may very well find that a few people can handle them all.

Secretary

- To handle correspondence, minutes of meetings, press releases, register of current members and potential helpers.
- To work with the Director on show plans and schedules.
- To make bookings for the Circus, arranging site facilities, transportation, parental permission, and time-tables.
- Getting insurance for club activities.
- To maintain contact with other groups, arranging visits and exchanges.
- To make sure everybody's on the bus!

Treasurer

- To keep the club solvent, by regulating income and expenditure.
- To coordinate fund-raising efforts.
- To negotiate performance fees
- To arrange equipment purchases when authorized by the committee.
- To pass the hat around at shows.

Publicity Chief

- To inform the press, radio and T.V. about Circus activities.
- To use the media for appeals, such as for costumes and props.
- To coordinate poster and handbill distribution for shows.
- To record the Club's progress on film, and make a scrapbook.
- To make and sell badges, T-shirts, and other fund-raising, publicity generating souvenirs.

- To compile a regular newsletter for parents, friends and other groups.
- To paint the van —and your own car if necessary —with the circus banner!

Wardrobe Supervisor

- To be responsible for costume and props.
- To collect, sew, patch and adapt clothes.
- To make sure the performers look clean and smart for shows.
- To encourage performers to create and look after their own costumes and equipment.
- To inspire local carpenters, knitters, painters, welders, etc., to lend their skills to the Circus.
- To keep a good stock of make-up and supervise its use.
- To be prepared to have your house taken over with circus gear!

Musical Director

- To get the best available musical accompaniment for the Circus, gathering and inspiring local talented people to work together occasionally, or, better still, form a band.
- To build a stock of "easy" instruments —kazoos, drums, horns and bells.
- To make tape-recordings for specific sequences, and ensure the presence of a reasonably good sound system.
- To do drum rolls —all the time!

Director

- To plan and coordinate the show.
- To arrange regular and effective rehearsals.
- To monitor and encourage the development of each individual member of the circus.
- To encourage other community members (dance and gymnastic teachers, professional entertainers, etc.) to join the team and help with coaching and rehearsals.
- To develop interest among the *parents* of the children in the circus.
- To make sure that the first five jobs are covered. Failing that, to do them yourself!

✴ A CIRCUS CLASS

Every circus group is different. In one, the children may need a rigidly organized weekly work-out; in another, the members may be more mature and able to work creatively and informally together, without a structure.

The following hints and suggestions relate to a circus group where you have 20 to 30 youngsters aged ten and up, two or three adults, and an indoor meeting place with basic equipment.

Storage of Equipment

Gymnastic mats should be rolled or stacked tidily after use.
Stilts are best stored upside down in wooden box.
Unicycles should *not* be just leaned on walls, as they will fall. It is possible to buy or make individual stands, but these take up floor space. It is best to *hang* them, either upside down on one peg, or, by saddle, between two pegs.
Juggling equipment—balls, clubs, etc.—is best kept in a box or tin trunk, along with loose stilt straps.
Costumes should be on racks or stowed neatly in trunks.

Layout of Rehearsal Hall

Stilts—near the stage, or table for mounting.
Unicycles—against a clear wall, for beginners. Park them upside down.
Gym mat—in the middle of the hall, away from obstructions.
Tightrope—parallel with one wall, about 6 feet from it, with bright ribbons tied to it so people don't walk or ride into it by mistake.
Juggling equipment—in a corner out of the way.
Trapeze and acrobatic harness—either over the central gym mat, or, if the room is big enough, away from everything else.

Organization

I tend to avoid whistle-blowing and shouting, but when I need everyone's attention, I clap, and ask everyone to sit on the mat. This is a central, finite and comfortable place. However, if you do this, be sure you have something significant and interesting to say or discuss, or you'll get less response next time.

Your ideal circus class should contain most of the following elements.

Preparation and warm-up.
Notices.
Demonstrations.
Technique work.
Game.
Rehearsal.
Clean-up.

| **Preparation and Warm-up** | The members should know where everything is kept, and should be able to lay out the equipment. They should change into gym shoes and gym clothes. As leader, take the group through a complete physical warm-up, including exercises for all parts of the body, teamwork, and balance control. |

This period should include basic gymnastic moves such as forward and backward rolls, crabs, and handstands. You should also use this period to work on activities like standing on shoulders and human pyramids. Structure the warm-up so that it ends on a note of cooperation and concentration rather than boisterous energy.

Notices

Before getting down to new work, bring the group together on the mat, check the roll, collect dues, and discuss upcoming events and arrangements. You should also have a bulletin board, and a system of notes to make sure information reaches your members and their parents.

Demonstration

Time permitting, I like to introduce a new idea or technique to the group each week. It may be a new juggling move I've picked up from a travelling friend, or an acrobatic sequence worked out by members of our group.

Occasionally, I'll show a film or slides of circus activity, or bring some books from my collection to interest the group.

This is also the opportunity to teach some elements of putting on a "show" —make-up drill, music-making, or assembling the "tent."

Technique Work

Now we split up into small groups to work on specific techniques. Juggling, tightrope and unicycling need no supervision, but there must be a competent adult with acrobatics, trapeze, and stilts.

Depending on time, the children will either stay with one activity or, at a signal from you, change once or more to the next activity.

Juggling

With the beginners, make sure they go through the learning stages outlined in the juggling chapter. Some people are simply not designed to juggle, and should not be forced into something that is frustrating and impossible.

With more advanced jugglers, encourage them to work in pairs, developing relationships and "plots." The good jugglers must also accept the responsibility of teaching beginners.

Throwing bean-bags about, although very tempting, is FORBIDDEN!

Stilts

An adult must be with every new learner. You are responsible for teaching correct strapping, and for the essential safety rules. Don't leave a beginner until he/she has performed all the first exercises confidently, and even then, each stilt walker must have a "spotter" — someone to catch them if they fall.

An adult must be with anyone trying Chinese stilts for the first time. Begin by holding her hands, and let her get used to moving about "on the spot," until she's prepared to let go, and then keep your hands high for her. Help her get used to taking steps *backwards* to keep balance.

Again, she should have a spotter until she is totally confident. Where possible, I encourage advanced stilt walkers to work outside, on grass. It leaves us more space in the hall, gives them a softer place to fall, gives them practice for parading in the wind, and attracts the attention of the public.

Acrobatics

The one big rule for children here is never cross the mat. Always check both ways when walking near it, in case someone is doing a run-up.

The rule for *you* is that you must have a qualified teacher, who can teach the moves, and who can teach you techniques to prevent accidents.

One or two of your better acrobats may work with your beginners on basic rolls, headstands and crabs. With others, you must revise everything they have done before, then make progress.

Encourage your members to make suggestions for new moves, but be cautious if an idea seems dangerous.

Unicycling

Teach beginners the techniques of mounting, and catching the uni. Then let them teach themselves and each other. Two important aids are the "parallel bar" technique (see p. 59) and side-by-side riding, with arms on each other's shoulders.

Competent riders should attempt to master a new move each time they attend the club. You should encourage healthy competition by highlighting individual achievements.

Tightrope

The tight-wire should not be above 2' high. An adult must check the rigging, as a taut wire is potentially dangerous. There should be a chair or step rather than having to step up onto the wire.

Only one person at a time on the wire. Members should wear thin-soled shoes.

Trapeze

It is *essential* to have either a competent spotter, or a safe "mechanic" or harness. Furthermore, there should be either a crash mat or doubled gym below the trapeze bar.

Unless you have a qualified instructor, restrict activities to those described in the trapeze chapter. For swinging and flying you'll need to attend a circus school.

Let your children work in short periods on the trapeze, as they may overestimate their own powers of strength and endurance.

Clown and Animal Routines

Children should be encouraged to work on their own sequences, provided that they realize that their efforts will probably need to be modified and shortened before they can go "public."

Game

To end the main session, we usually have a game of unicycle "tag," or a catching game with juggling balls. Then the children pack up the equipment.

Rehearsal

I find that it is a good thing to have a specific rehearsal with a smaller, advanced team for half an hour or so after the main group has left. There is a good atmosphere in the hall, a feeling of warmth and achievement, and a sense among those who remain of being the chosen few, with the responsibility to produce something new.

CIRCUS IN SCHOOLS

When I was training as an elementary school teacher, the fashion in educational circles was for "project teaching." Get the class interested in one suitable topic, and explore it with them in every possible way —analytically, historically, mathematically, environmentally, creatively, etc.

I remember cycling to school on a tandem in those days, and using it as the central theme of my project. The poor children had to play music on the spokes, analyze the rust content, research the origins, explain the gearing system, and use the shape as inspiration for stained glass windows! After about three weeks of the dreaded tandem, some boys in my class kindly offered to give me the cost of the bus fare.

It's a pity I didn't know much about the Circus in those days. Today, there's hardly any subject I can think of which gives more scope for education, both practical and theoretical, in every aspect, than Circus. If I were to go back to school-teaching, and if my class was ready for a big, long-term project on Circus, these are some of the many ideas I could choose from:

Physical Education: Acrobatics

Forward Roll
Backward Roll
Wheelbarrow
Crab Walk
Cartwheel
Hand stand / Squat

The variety of circus acrobatics makes it much more suitable for schools than Olympic gymnastics. By its very nature, Olympic gymnastics is exclusive. It demands a certain shape of girl, emphasizing a high degree of back suppleness (and a gross distortion of the pelvic/lower back region). The "aesthetic" element of girls' gymnastics, which seems to be dictated by the 1950's style of the Eastern-bloc, seems to me to be a denial of the inherent beauty of movement which girls and young women are capable of.

In men's gymnastics, it is very encouraging to see group work and circus-type acrobatics becoming fashionable again, even at the highest level.

But I would begin this type of work at the lowest level. In the first years of school, children should be encouraged to continue their natural inclination to tumble about together, developing partner and group skills, rather than separating them, and highlighting the capabilities of some and the inadequacies of others.

In Circus acrobatics, there is scope for suppleness and grace, but there is also a demand for solidity, and buffoonery. Of course, each child must learn something of each element, in order to feel what their colleagues are doing, but each should be able to make the best of his/her natural talents.

Unicycle

Ra/ K ?
Skateboard Scooter
Skateboard,
Off Center bike,
scooter

There are elementary schools in America and Japan where unicycling is on the curriculum. The teachers there (who are probably one-wheel fanatics like me) have clearly seen the advantages to physical development of this sport. The U.S. government gave a major grant to promote unicycles in schools.

19

Teachers report that the unicycle has a positive influence on personality development, allowing the child to overcome shyness, gain self-confidence, and build a positive attitude towards meeting difficult challenges. I know that there's no better way to work up a sweat than the quick stop/start/turn/twist movement of uni-tag.

In parts of the U.S.A. Uni-ball (basketball on unicycles) is very popular. It depends on the ability to stand on the pedals, holding the saddle between the legs, and just lift the body, bringing hands down *below* foot level to pick the ball off the ground. This beats touching your toes any day. Other games include Uni-hockey, Uni-dodge ball, Uni-tennis and Uni-sumo wrestling!

Juggling

Scarves
One/Two Hand
Club Swinging
Roll A Bola
Balancing Poles,
etc,

In school sports, great emphasis is laid on the ability to hurl, spin and catch one ball at a time. It's a logical extension of this skill to deal with two, three or more balls at a time — i.e., juggling. Furthermore, just as dance and gymnastics are increasingly popular as non-aggressive, non-contact sports, so juggling is a personal sport, one in which you are competing against no one except gravity and your own slow reflexes — and defying both!

Art

Posters
Scenes
Flyers
Face paints
Make up
Costumes
etc,

The great days of the Circus — 1880 to 1920 — were characterized by an emphasis on design. Circus posters of that era are rightly regarded as tokens of the age. No art historian of the period can ignore the importance of the style which developed then — photographic and cartoon-like scenes depicted inside Baroque scrolls and frames. It was the great age of color lithography, never likely to be repeated since the coming of photography. Those huge posters depicting twelve or more highly decorated scenes, each with its own extravagantly worded caption, which were the fore-runners of today's comic strips and cartoons, have rightly been accepted into the portals of fine art and design.

So the art teacher has a wealth of material to draw on in posters alone. But there is also the design of costumes, wagons, ring doors and props to be considered.

Finally, school children should have opportunity to shape the design on that most bizarre canvas, the human face. It's possible to buy non-allergenic, water-based face paints now, so teachers can safely let their children loose on the task of designing clown and other make-ups on themselves and each other.

Music

Kazoos
Slide whistle
Drums
Shakers
Rhythm Sticks, etc

Starting with a simple drum, a circus band can be built up with almost any number and combination of instruments. An imaginative musical director can develop every conceivable type of music to accompany a circus, from primeval rhythmic drumming to jazz to the most sophisticated chamber music. All will be reflected by the different acts in the ring.

In teaching drama, I have always been conscious that even here, there is the possibility that some members of the class are being left out. While most of the class are expanding emotionally, learning self-expression, self control and creative ways of inter-relating within the group, there are always a few children who will not get involved. These tend to be the extroverts, like you and me, who would rather lead than be led, and the introverts, who cannot cope with the stress of putting themselves on the line, body and soul.

I turned from drama to circus largely because of a growing awareness that things were getting too easy for me as a drama teacher. I had learned so many ways to manipulate a group, and to get them to work in ways which neither I nor they understood, but no one questioned. In fact, it was too easy to betray their confidence. So I looked for methods of working in drama where I was less the arbiter.

I found the answer in circus techniques. Here, I could demonstrate the beginnings of the process — whether in juggling, stilts, or whatever — and the children took it from there.

There's no other medium I know in which the pupil can get demonstrably better than the teacher in such a short time — especially when the teacher initially shows an ability like unicycling which seems super-human. As the children in the Pilton Circus will tell you, it's a great thrill to be better than your teacher, especially after going through school without excelling at anything.

And, take it from me, as a teacher, there's no thrill to compare with seeing a confirmed "non-achiever" suddenly achieve something, fight to reach my own standard, overtake, and then go ahead to levels I can never hope to reach.

But back to drama. Once a quiet, introverted boy has learned, say, to walk on stilts, he must do something about it. He is accepted into a group which previously would have rejected him. With the group he must learn timing, choreography, self-presentation. Eventually he may find himself, almost accidentally, producing drama.

That extrovert in the class, who is really a shy boy behind a brash mask, can now use that brashness as a virtue. You as teacher can relax; no longer do you have to put him down, or fight him for the position of head of the class. You can *use* him. You have a natural ringmaster. That group of naughty girls, instead of focusing their mischief on *you,* now become the clowns, and can channel all their ingenuity, charm, and cunning against your ringmaster.

The Circus becomes a stylization of all the relationships, the plots and subplots that are continuously running through the class. You can finally stand back and let it happen!

STREET CIRCUS AND BUSKING

Most circus acts started on the street, and today many are going back. In many cities, in the streets, shopping arcades, parks and subways you'll see musicians, jugglers, white-faced mimes, and, occasionally, fire-eaters and escapologists. I hope you'll drop some money in their hats — if they're good. If they're no good, they won't last long.

Busking is usually illegal. However, some performers obtain licenses, and some streets and squares are designated busking areas, like the famous Place Pompidou in Paris. There, and in the Covent Garden Market, London, one has the chance to see many different ways of collecting money from the public.

- A blind violinst scrapes away all day, with a cloth cap on the ground, nodding his thanks whenever he hears a coin clink on the others. (Never put down an empty hat . . . cash attracts cash.)

- A crazy unicyclist weaves unbelievably in and out of the traffic to the consternation of the drivers, but the delight of the pedestrians, who stop and form a crowd. The unicyclist doesn't stop, but two pretty girls, wearing the same colors as the performer, move among the crowd, collecting money in tins on his behalf.

- Two jugglers perform a fast, comic routine, and draw a sizeable circle of on-lookers. After about 5 minutes of action, without once acknowledging the audience, they begin to talk:

  > Bill: How are we doing?
  > Jim: I think they like it.
  > Bill: How will we know?
  > Jim: We'll see how much they give us.
  > Bill: When?
  > Jim: Now. (Stops juggling) I'll collect for you.

He moves around the audience, collecting donations, smiling a lot, and saying, "Isn't he good — for a beginner?" Then, "Okay, Bill, I'll take over, and we'll see what they think of me." Bill now "bottles" and thus they manager to milk the audience twice.

- Further on, a tough-looking man in a leopard skin has a mighty pile of chains, padlocks and nails. He has a large crowd around him, waiting, watching. He has a plate, seemingly full of silver coins, but he's not happy.

  > "No, my friends, not yet. I'm a professional. I intend to entertain you and amaze you, but I must earn a living. Thank you, sir. We're nearly there. No, sorry, Madam, I only take silver coins, not brown ones, thank you. Just three more, and we're ready to begin. One, two, thank you, sir, yes? Three! That's it, let us begin."

He then performs his escape act, which *is* good, and leaves the audience quite satisfied. As they disperse to tell their friends, he begins collecting his fee for the next performance.

If you intend to take your Children's Circus on the streets, you'll probably need a permit from the police. You'll also need a special dispensation to collect money in a public place. However, if you are performing at a fair, or in a back-yard, the audience will probably want to contribute something, and you should make it easy for them.

As Ringmaster, I usually come out just before the next to last act. "Ladies and Gentlemen, I hope you've enjoyed our show so far. There's more to come, but first may I tell you a bit about the Hometown Suitcase Circus. We are run entirely by volunteers, and the children themselves contribute to the club funds to buy equipment for the circus. We are currently aiming to collect $100.00 for two new junior unicycles. I hope you can help. During the next act, our clowns will pass among you with hats, bags and Wellington boots. Please give generously. Thank you. Now, on with the show!"

The same clowns will station themselves at the exit at the end of the show, and almost certainly make another significant collection. Be sure to smile and thank each donor specially.

You may decide to take a group from your circus to perform in a public place to advertise your show, or to provide a news story, or just to give the public a free show. Be sure to check the following points:

- Don't obstruct the street or sidewalk.
- Don't block access to shops, which would turn the tradesmen's goodwill into bad.
- Be sure the ground is safe for stilts and unicycles — not wet and slippery.
- Don't plan an acrobatic *rolling* sequence, unless you have a mat or grass.
- Don't use bouncy juggling balls unless you're an excellent juggler.
- Take a length of bunting for the front row of the audience to hold, if it is necessary to keep them back.
- Don't take a lot of loose props, and keep an eye on those you have. The public is generally kind to street performers, but you should avoid providing the temptation to steal your gear.

Have a short show, with a good, definite ending, and encourage applause. If the police move you on, don't argue; just smile and cooperate.

THE PROFESSIONAL CIRCUS

I face a group of 30 children in Edinburgh, who have been working with me on a Suitcase Circus over 12 weeks, and have already performed publicly three times. "Hands up — those who have seen a real circus."

20 hands go up.

"What circus have you seen, Cathy?"

"I don't know, it was on the telly."

"Okay, take your hands down if you've only seen one on the telly." Only six hands remain up!

I went to a *real* touring circus, probably eight times during my childhood. There are few adults who've never had the experience. But today's children are missing out! There are fewer touring shows, tickets seem to cost so much more, parents are apathetic, and there's the dreaded television.

So I took this group to the circus. Their response was very interesting. Some were totally hypnotized by the glamor, the lights and the smells of the show. Others were intrigued by the rigging and equipment — "so much better than ours." Some were full of admiration for the Ringmaster, whose timing and sense of authority were so meticulous, or the drummer, who managed to provide every act with the required roll, crash and tinkle, exactly on cue, while never losing the rhythm of the music.

Several of the children were frankly critical. The trapeze act was elementary — nothing that we don't do at the club — except that it was 40 feet up! "The unicyclist stepped off a ladder, while our Dougie can do a climbing monkey mount!"

These last reactions are just what I was hoping for. I pointed out that the professionals have managed to impress the crowd, and draw applause, by doing their acts with STYLE. Even if we at the circus club have learned some techniques, we are not true performers until we can wow an audience like that.

But I agreed with the harsher critics that some of the acts were *bad*. The clowns weren't funny, and they had no skills; the stilt walker just shuffled on and shuffled off again; the tumblers could have been more precise with their timing; some of the costumes were tatty, and the follow-spot operator was half asleep.

Professional circus folk aren't used to this sort of criticism, and some of them resent it. A small circus owner in Scotland told me that I "have no right to be teaching circus secrets to members of the audience." I take this accusation very seriously, and answer it with the following points:
- Amateurs never did professionals any harm — in soccer, baseball, music or drama. In fact, the reverse is true, and the true amateur is the best and most appreciative fan.
- A critical audience will identify the dross, and those small, bad, tenting shows which give circus a bad name will have to leave the field to the higher quality companies.

- I don't teach secrets, and when children ask me how a performer eats fire, and walks on glass, or saws a lady in half, I simply tell them it's a professional circus secret which they don't have the right to know yet.
- But I do teach skills. So now, when a juggler comes to town, he may be pleasantly surprised when his really difficult tricks — like a 6-ball shower or a 5-club cascade get a special round of real applause from our kids. They now know the difference between good juggling and mediocre juggling, and that's no bad thing.
- Circus is no longer a closed shop — a family business. Many circus children are going outside the world of the shows to earn a secure living elsewhere. So where will tomorrow's stars come from? We provide the answer. From the streets of our home towns. There are children I've seen in local circuses in Britain who would be a credit to any circus family, and in the current state of employment, a young person could do a lot worse than join a circus. He'll be in the vanguard of our only growing industry — the leisure industry.

A Community/Professional Collaboration

Early in 1980, I was working in Cardiff, Wales, with the Splott Children's Circus, which had been founded the previous summer by a graduate of our Scottish Circus School. In the Cardiff Pavilion for that winter season was Mary Chipperfield's Circus Wirld — a big show, featuring mostly animals, but with several excellent acts of human skills, including Tommy Fossett, of a famous old British circus family.

Mr. Fossett, truly a member of the British circus aristocracy, was kind enough to visit us at work, He gave me, and some of our young performers, some vital and unforgettable things, like keeping your head up at all times on the high unicycle, and, when juggling clubs, keeping them low, and thrusting the handles away, to give them such a spin that they've got no choice but to thud into the other hand. Seeing Mr. Fossett, in his street clothes, demonstrating his magical ability with the clubs for 30 kids in a cold church hall, I realized that contact with the professionals must not be avoided. We must do all we can to let our children experience this level of skill and commitment found only in the traditional touring circuses.

Two days later, our children were backstage at this Cardiff Pavilion — with camels, elephants, horses, and a crocodile! Tommy Fossett had given up his 8-minute clown spot so that the Splott children could perform in a real, full-sized sawdust ring, in front of a real paying audience — and the television cameras.

As the ringmaster announced the "Splott Children's Circus" our stilt walkers skipped out round the ring, followed by the unicyclists, who darted in and out between their legs.

The acrobats followed them, laying out their mats, and going into a routine which included back-somersaults by Richard. He was a mere reserve for the Welsh Junior Gymnastics Squad, but with us, he was top of the bill. The jugglers, clowns, plate-spinners and the monkeys all did their bit during that busy, magical 8 minutes . . . and the audience, and Mary Chipperfield's company, were delighted.

That generous act by Tommy Fossett ensured that in Cardiff there are at least 30 more families who are now hooked on the circus, and who will never miss the opportunity to go along when the Circus comes to town.

ACROBATICS

Acrobatics, or tumbling, has been part of street and court entertainment throughout history, all over the world. It is the most basic of all the circus skills, as in its purest form it needs no equipment, and can be done by one person.

Equipment

You'll almost certainly need a gym mat. The best is an "agility mat"—15' or more long × 4' wide, made of foam rubber covered with canvas or PVC. Or use smaller mats, usually 6' × 4', which have the advantage that you can design different patterns, but the disadvantage that they tend to slip apart.

A trampette or mini-trampoline will be a boon to a tumbling act, but must be used only with a qualified coach.

A crash-mat—usually 6' × 8' × 1' thick—is very useful for landing from high pyramids, and fast group-tumbling sequences, especially comedy tumbling. However, it must be used with caution, as a tumbler can land awkwardly and fall off it onto the hard floor.

A spotting belt, which is a belt 3" to 4" wide with loops at each side, is useful for spotting backflips and somersaults.

Your tumblers should wear gym shoes, or bare feet—never just socks—and either tights, shorts, or loose clothes like track suits.

Forward Roll

Squat, facing the mat, and bend forward, placing first the hands on mat, then the back of your head. As you roll, your feet leave the ground behind you, and reach the ground in front of you. DON'T push the ground with your hands as you get up, but reach the hands forward. Keep tucked throughout. Some children just *can't* do this straight. I make them think of their spine as a machine for painting white lines down the middle of the road, and I show them the line on the mat. This usually helps.

Variations

Try with no hands—or balancing a ball in each hand. Slowly squat, and put the back of the neck down first.

High Roll

Go over a partner bending down, sideways on, over a chair, or through a hoop.

Run and leap forward horizontally, arms outstretched, Superman-style. When you're landing, put both hands down firmly, and curl into a forward roll.

Dive Forward Roll

In the Suitcase Circus, this simple move can provide a great climactic finish to a show, with leapers flying over first one, then two, three, four, up to our personal record of sixteen prone bodies. We call this the DEATH DIVE.

"You've seen us juggling balls, clubs, handkerchiefs, and knives, and now, with their very own bodies — the Human Jugglers."

Here's a delightfully simple, continuous routine for three acrobats, involving a JUMP, a FORWARD ROLL, and a TURN.

Human Juggling

On a 12' mat, A and B at each end face center. C stands center facing A. C jumps over nothing. lands, and forward rolls, then turns. A jumps over C's roll, lands and rolls, then turns.

B jumps over A's roll, lands and rolls towards C (who has turned), and turns.

C jumps over B, lands, and rolls, then turns. A jumps over C's roll, etc., etc., etc., JUMP, ROLL, TURN, JUMP, ROLL, TURN.

The jump must be a high, star jump — arms and legs out. The roll must be tight, the turn quick. The move is made more dramatic if A and B are chasing C, who keeps darting over and under his pursuers.

Human Juggling Marathons are a favorite for Circus Festivals. The best performance I know of is 80 jumps before collapse.

Backward Roll

Back to the mat, squat, sit and roll over. Take your hands to either side of your head, to PUSH the mat as your head turns. Then back onto your feet.

Variations

Push up to a handstand at the critical moment, taking off and landing on your feet.

Try back-roll into headstand. Tricky.

Comic fall. Head goes to one side as you go over, supported by bent arms, and you land flat on your front.

Headstand
(Worm's Eye View)

Place top of head and palms of hands on the floor in an equal triangle, then walk up toward them. When you feel ready to roll, STRAIGHTEN the back, and let the legs rise into the air. To avoid falling, keep a significant weight on the hands.

When you've achieved a good firm headstand, open and close your legs, raise and lower them, cycle them. Hold a headstand position, legs apart, while someone does a dive forward roll through the V.

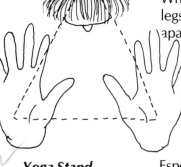

Yoga Stand

Especially impressive if legs are in the lotus position.

Forearm Stand

Quite difficult, but impressive if you can backward roll into it.

Handstands

Practice against a wall, or with a partner facing you, ready to take your legs on his shoulder. Place hands 1' from the wall, or either side of your partner's forward foot, and kick upwards with legs.

- Keep arms straight.
- Hands not splayed, but directly under shoulders.
- Head looking up, towards the wall, or supporter.
- Legs together, straight, toes pointing.

Walking on Hands

When your handstand is strong, try walking, by arching the back, and leaning the legs in the direction you wish to go.

Walking-on-hands speed, distance, and endurance races are another feature at Circus Festivals.

Cartwheels	Move to the mat, facing front, then with right foot forward, both hands up, turn the hips sideways to the right and make tracks hand, hand, foot, foot straight down the line, to end standing, facing the left side of the mat.
	When you can do it straight, learn to do it curved. Cartwheel around the ring, facing *outwards*.
Arab Spring	Approach the mat as if for a cartwheel, but place two hands almost simultaneously, legs up, twist in the air, and land two feet together so you're facing the way you came from. This is the preparation for a back flip.
Handspring	Run towards the mat, one skip-step, place both hands on the mat, continue quickly up into a handstand, but with your head still up facing forward. Then as your feet pass over your head, release the tension and continue over to land on your feet.
	When learning this, you should have a competent spotter kneeling, with his arm supporting the small of your back.

For the individual moves that follow, you must have a qualified instructor with you. So please don't read these descriptions as instructions.

Back Flip	Lean forwards while facing backwards. Hurl yourself over backwards. Land on your hands and continue over to land on your feet.
Back Somersault	Like a back flip, except you bunch up, and the hands don't touch the ground. You land on your feet.
Front Somersault	With a run up, jump high off, both feet together, tuck up tight, turn in the air, and land on your feet.
One-Arm Cartwheel	Either the first or second arm.
No-Arm Cartwheel	Lots of spring, and lots of height.

So far we have dealt with individual movement and balance, both of which are essentials of the acrobatic act. But there's another quality found particularly in young people which is of great value to a circus act. I mean the ability to bend themselves into astonishing shapes.

The Crab is the most obvious. Either push up from the ground, or gently fall over backwards, or forward handstand into crab. For the circus, don't stretch out with straight legs, but get your feet nearer to your hands, to make a high curve, which is stronger than you think. A small child who is *lifted* up can stand on your pelvic bones without causing you undue discomfort.

A popular Suitcase Circus move is to have a little clown or monkey crawl along inside a tunnel of crabs, while another, holding a helper's hand, walks across the top. See page 17.

Walkovers. Once you have mastered the crab, and handstand into a crab, try the walkover. Your back must be supported, as you handstand, then bring one foot to the floor, and release your hands as your foot can take the body's weight, then stand.

For the back walkover, again with support, you lean over backwards, leading with hands and head with one leg following high. When your hands reach the ground, release the leg on the ground. It follows the first one over to a standing position.

Contortion. Explore the possibilities yourself, but they include crossing your legs in your lap, behind your neck, and even behind your shoulders. Make sure you are well warmed up before you start contortions, and never push yourself beyond the pain threshhold.

Pair Work: Shoulder Sit

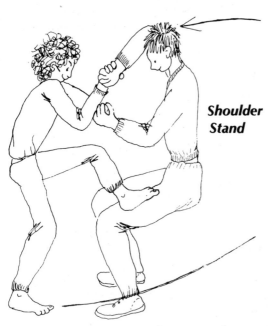

The neatest way to get up is for the rider to stand, legs apart, and the lifter to put his head between her legs from behind, and lift with a straight back. This is how to lift for giants (page 52). Other ways up involve a handstand, a leap-frog, hands-stirrups and leg-steps. Try these yourself — but have a spotter.

Shoulder Stand

This is very useful for pyramids, for short parades, and for fixing bunting on high poles. The best way up is the leg step.

- Grasp left hands.
- Grasp right hands, across palm, with thumbs down.
- You squat straight, and rider puts left foot on your upper thigh.
- She steps up to put her right foot on your right shoulder. As she leaves the ground, you move your arms to the right in a vertical plane across your head.

- As you push up with both hands, she puts her left foot on your left shoulder.
- One at a time, you release her hands, and hold calves, (fingers behind) so her shins rest on your head. She stands straight, only her knees slightly bent. The spotter must stand behind. If she falls, you *must* let go her legs, and she will either jump down forward, or slide down behind you, to land on her feet.

Pyramids

Pyramids, or tableaux, are based on the shoulder stand. There are infinite combinations, and they make an excellent end to an acrobatic routine, or the whole show. For a big group, have the highest feature in the center, and arrange the others in diminishing height symmetrically on either side, and in front, in headstands, crabs, splits and other poses.

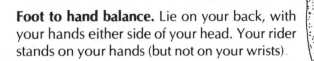

Foot to hand balance. Lie on your back, with your hands either side of your head. Your rider stands on your hands (but not on your wrists).

You put your legs in the air, she holds your feet. She jumps; you push, and straighten your arm vertically. She straightens with arms by her side. You keep her balanced.

Be careful coming down. If she lifts one foot, ALL the weight will be on your remaining arm, which will collapse. So she must step off to the side. Alternatively, let her sit on your feet, then as you hold her ankles, she back bends, puts her hands on the ground. You let go, and give her a *gentle* push, over, and back onto her feet.

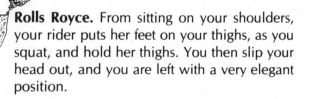

Rolls Royce. From sitting on your shoulders, your rider puts her feet on your thighs, as you squat, and hold her thighs. You then slip your head out, and you are left with a very elegant position.

Head/shoulder stand. Lie on your back, knees up, hands up. She rests her hands on your knees, and leans forward to let you support her shoulders. She goes up to a handstand— *straightening her arms.* From this position, she may be able to release her arms one at a time, to wind them around your arms. Yor have an arm-to-arm stand. It's important that in this, and the hand-to-foot, she remains rigid, and let's *you* do the balancing, as you would with a broomstick.

31

Two Person Cartwheel	Not easy, but very effective. It depends on a wide spread of the legs, and considerable strength in the arms.
Rolling Handstand	A slow process, and a lot of hard work. Partners are about the same height. A stands firm. B, behind him, handstands, to bring his feet onto A's shoulders. A squats slightly, holds B's ankles, and bends forward, so their backs are close together, and pulls B over onto his feet. B takes a step forward, and A goes up into a handstand behind B, etc.
Rolling Shoulder Hold	A squats slightly, his arms straight down, with his hands pointing backward, palms upwards. B bends low to put his shoulders in A's hands, and lifts his arms under and up, to grasp A's shoulders in the same way. B then kicks up, to get his legs in the air, and is left hanging on A's back.

A then bends forward, B's feet come to the ground, and A kicks upwards to take the upside-down position. B bends, A comes over, etc.

This is difficult, but possible with two good acrobats of the same size.

Suggested Routine

The essential quality of the acrobatic act is surprising change of pace and shape. For instance,
1. The troupe enters, leap-frogging around the ring, finally stopping in a circle, facing outward for applause.
2. At a given signal, they turn inward for a rolling, springing and cart-wheeling sequence across the mats.
3. They follow this by a display of flexibility, with slow walkovers and crabs.
4. Take this a stage further with a display of contortion.
5. Change pace by announcing an attempt at your circus's human juggling record. This is even more exciting with two teams on parallel mats, with the crowd shouting out the number of jumps.
6. Now, let each member of the troupe come across the mat with their specialty: comic backward roll, one-arm cartwheel, handspring. End with the most impressive, like an arab spring and two back flips.
7. Then, as the drum rolls, all the acrobats form a tableau —pyramid, crabs and splits. Applause!
8. Jump down, take a bow, and cartwheel off.

ANIMAL SHOW (FAKE)

Little Clown: "And now, Ladies and Gentlemen, at enormous expense, we bring to this arena, for the first time in this country, the biggest gorilla in captivity—the truly amazing King Congo!"

A tiny child in a monkey suit scampers out through the ring door, runs between the large Ringmaster's legs, and plucks at his coat, asking to be picked up.

The Ringmaster, in mock anger, chases the monkey, *and* the little clown, right round the ring, back to starting position. The monkey cowers in the middle while the Ringmaster shouts at the clown. "What is the meaning of this? You said it was a gigantic gorilla. Where did you get that miserable creature? I've a good mind to —"

A tap on his shoulder. He turns to face, eyeball to bloodshot eyeball, two full-size adult gorillas, male and female. They frogmarch him round the ring and dump him on the ground, where the little monkey proceeds to jump on his stomach and sit on his face. The clown hurries off.

Meanwhile one gorilla—the male—wanders into the audience, picks up a little girl, and sits her on his lap, grooming her hair.

The female, in a fit of rage, carefully puts the little girl aside, grabs her mate by the head, and hurls him into the ring. The tom-toms thunder as the two mighty beasts clash and fall, fighting as energetically (and as carefully) as television wrestlers.

Eventually they both collapse, and lie immobile on their backs. The drums fall silent. The little clown comes out from hiding and, with the little monkey, creeps cautiously toward the apes. With much pushing and cowering, they eventually summon up enough courage to tickle the great hairy stomachs of the gorillas. The beasts twitch, turn, and finally get up and run away from their tiny tormentors. The little ones chase them round the ring, finally jumping on their backs. They run around once more and leave.

This is a sure-fire routine, combining suspense, surprise, putting down the big guys, and triumph of the little ones. It is, essentially, a human plot, but it is improved immeasurably by good ape-suits, masks, and, above all, good movement.

Ape Costumes	Try to avoid the one-piece ape suits, which always have pathetically baggy legs. The best ape suits are made in three parts of dark, shaggy fur fabric: • Trousers, which continue into feet. • A leotard-type top, with back fastening, and gloves attached (normal black woolen gloves, with fur backs). • A complete head, with latex face and ears.
Ape Pantomime	In my experience, the best way to ape an ape is to ape a chimp. Bend the knees outward, feet close together, but tilted out, so you walk on the outside of your feet. Stick your bottom out, but arch the back to keep your head up. Let the arms hang long, but not stiff.

A chimp's footsteps are one in front of the other, so walk as if along a branch, holding arms up for balance. Remember that an ape is more comfortable resting on its knuckles, and that standing is unnatural. It should only rise to nearly full human height in order to beat its chest in anger.

Most wild animals, including apes, know the value of stillness, and will freeze at the first hint of danger, then move quickly to another position and freeze again. Practice this, and other aspects of chimp behavior, to achieve a credible act.

This is one of many "Fake" animal acts which enhance your circus a great deal, and give scope to members of your group not especially talented in other directions. Here's something to do with any number of under-6 year olds:

Lions and Tigers

Make up the children with black noses and whiskers, and if possible, striped or spotted cat suits. Teach them the secret words:

"Simba"	Go to sleep.
"Uppah!"	Get fierce. Show your claws, teeth and eyes — and ROAR!
"Downah!"	Neutral position. Move slowly around, grooming yourselves and sniffing each other.
"Tableau!"	Get to the positions we rehearsed (a posed group, with some kneeling, some with front paws on their backs, and some lying down. All growl and paw the air).
"Kittens!"	*Attack* the trainer.

34

You then introduce your unique pride of lions, leopard, tigers and panthers. They enter (on all fours) and jump through hoops, and sit on chairs at your command. You demonstrate your mastery over these savage big-cats by "Uppahs!" and "Downahs!" and "Tableau!" and eventually a "Simba!" As they all lie asleep, you turn to your audience. "And so, ladies and gentlemen, I have tamed these ferocious beasts of the jungle, and under my command, they become like little *kittens*. See how they lie there peacefully, just like cats in front of the — HELP!" By this time the children have crept up and are attacking you en masse.

"Simba! Simba!" They sleep again. You repeat this sort of thing two or three times, until finally they chase you round the ring and out.

Snake Charming

This is one of the great traditional mysteries of the Orient. But our researchers at Suitcase Circus have finally solved the mystery. The turbaned fakir sits before a wicker basket, and as his weird tune, and his flute, rise higher and higher, the lid opens and reveals the menacing head of the dreaded spitting cobra. It sways from side to side, as the fakir trembles with alarm. Finally, he stops playing, and the deadly reptile springs out of the basket, and slithers across the grass at the feet of the fleeing, screaming dervish — a truly frightening and bewildering act.

We can now reveal the secret of the mystey which has puzzled audiences for generations. See diagram above. Deadly spitting cobras are inexpensively available at your local joke shop.

This two-person, four-legged beast is a traditional element in the English pantomime. It is found in many other parts of the world, notably in the Far East, taking the form of a hairy dog, lion, or dragon. The costume usually comes in three parts. Each person has a pair of trousers. Then comes the main section, made of stiff cloth, often over a framework of plastic. The head section, worn above the front person's head, is carefully made, often with moving parts like eyeballs and jaws. These can be controlled by the front person's hand.

The person in the back end of the horse has the unenviable job of maintaining a bent back position, with his hands on the waist of the person in front. It helps if these two are friends! In England, to be the "back of a horse" is to be at the very bottom of the theatrical ladder.

Ideas for a scene with the horse will come to you naturally. He is a comic creature, and as such is capable of pathos. He can sulk and lose his temper, just as graphically as he can march, dance, and scratch himself. Small children can ride on his back. He in turn can ride on other people. I've even known a pantomime reindeer to do a trampoline act!

From the principle of 2 legs + 2 legs = 4 legs, you can go on to more ambitious projects, which I have used successfully with competent stiltwalkers—a pantomime giraffe and a pantomime elephant. Footed stilts should be worn, and the front person should be strong enough to control a large head structure, while the back person should take care to walk in the correct step pattern for a large quadruped.

The Circus Ostrich

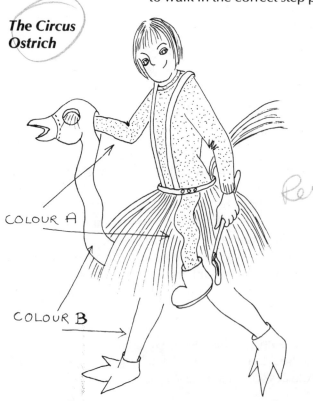

COLOUR A

COLOUR B

To see several of these lovely beasts in a street parade—like the "French Ostrich Legionnaires" of Natural Theate Company of Bath, England—is an inspiring and hilarious sight.

You must practice a long loping stride, with the head and neck undulating as you walk.

An alternative control to the "muppet" type head would be stiff wire reins to the head, enabling you to raise, lower and turn it.

ANIMAL SHOWS (REAL)

By all means, use your domestic pets in your Suitcase Circus, *if they enjoy it*. There's a fashionable feeling currently against seeing lions, elephants, bears, etc. "degraded" in the ring. But *domestic* animals are different, as they have been bred for thousands of years specifically to act "unnaturally" to please us.

A Dog Act

Find out what the animal likes to do and work your act around that behavior. For example, my friend's dog, Wag, likes to jump for sticks. I hold a stick up and he jumps for it. With practice, I'll get him to jump through a hoop. As a finale, I hold the stick in front of me. He jumps at it, and into my arms, or, better still, he jumps onto me and we both fall over!

A Duck Act

I have a pet duck, MacDonald, who has proved totally immune to training of any sort. But there are two things he can do, and I've coordinated them into an act.

1. He has a passion for my red leather boots, and he nibbles at them incessantly as I walk along.
2. A duck (any duck) will be still if it is laid down carefully on its back.

I "hypnotize" the duck with lots of mumbo-jumbo talk as I place him carefully on his back. Stepping back, I tell him that he will wake up when I snap my fingers, and he will be in love with my boots. I then snap my fingers. If nothing happens, at least it's funny, but even funnier if he finally stands up and passionately kisses my boots.

A Parade

If your Suitcase Circus is a one-day event, then a marvelous act is a Pets Parade. Have the children in the company—and the audience—go home and bring back their pets. Then they simply walk around the ring, leading or carrying their dogs, cats, hamsters, gerbils, stick-insects, etc.

JUGGLING

First, a true story:

Down in the Sinai Desert, an unwilling conscript in the Israeli Army had the job of guarding eggs. Exactly what or who threatened the eggs, he wasn't quite sure, but he obeyed orders. Eggs get very boring after a while, so what more natural than that he should begin to juggle them. First one at a time, then two, and then, several hundred smashed eggs later, he achieved 3-EGG JUGGLING!

Eventually he was demobilized, but like any good Israeli, he never forgot his army training. Back in his apartment in Jerusalem he continued to juggle eggs. He toiled away at 4-egg juggling, working in the tiled kitchen, where the frequent mistakes could be cleaned up easily. But his life was getting very expensive, and omelettes monotonous, so he racked his brain to think of a quick way to improve his catching technique.

Suddenly, the answer came to him. He took his four eggs out of the kitchen, across the hall, into the lounge, and stood right in the center of his highly prized and very expensive carpet! He began to juggle—very cautiously at first, and then with more and more confidence. His catching improved dramatically that night. He is now a very fine juggler.

There is another way to improve your catching. IMPROVE YOUR THROWING!

There are two types of juggling:

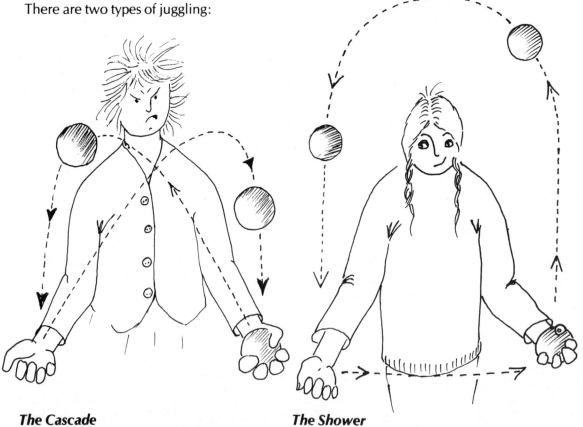

The Cascade
with 3, 5, 7 or other odd number of objects

The Shower
with any number of objects—1, 2, 3, 4 or more

The Shower

Whenever you see a picture of a juggler, it looks like this. It's called the low-level, 6 ball shower, and it is impossible!

To shower three balls, take two in your best hand, one in the other. Toss no. 1, then 2, and immediately flick 3 across to your throwing hand, and let it follow no. 2. Catching hand receives1, and flicks it across to folow 3, ad infinitum.

At first, your throws must be high—at least a foot over your head. But you'll get better (lower) or cleverer (still high, but with 4 or 5 balls). The essential rule is to maintain even throwing, so that the catching can look after itself.

The Cascade

That's all I'll tell you about the shower. The cascade is much more versatile, and for most people, easier.* I teach the three-ball cascade like this:

**Lesson One:
One Ball**

A juggler must get a good posture. Stand comfortably. Relax your body. Hold the hands in front of the elbows, and keep them there, approximately. Toss the ball from one hand to the other. It should leave the center of your hand—not the ends of your fingers. That way may look more casual, but it's too variable, and at this stage, you need constants. The ball should go head height, and land in the other hand, which should not have moved.

Now do it with the eyes closed. This drives you mad. Get a rhythm going first, with your eyes open, then close them and carry on.

Three ways to cheat:

- Lift both hands to head level, so you're only tossing it a few inches.
- Keep your hands low, and lob it in front of your stomach.
- Peep.

If you do any of these you're disqualified, and must leave the chapter immediately. Meanwhile, for those serious students still with us:

*An encouraging word to adults here. In my experience, juggling is the only "Suitcase Circus" skill which adults learn faster than children. The ideal learner is about 20 years old, of medium build, and is a piano-playing mathematician. If you are, I can guarantee to teach you juggling in 5 minutes! Mathematicians quickly grasp the logic and simple beauty of the moves, and, as for pianists, well, juggling is just the vamping on an upside-down keyboard. Try it!

Lesson Two:
Two Balls

This is the tricky bit. Remember that each ball passes, in front of your face, to the other hand. Now. THROW THROW CATCH CATCH. If your rhythm is THROW, THROW CATCH, CATCH, then your second throw is going too late. If it is THROW, THROW CATCH! I bet you're lifting your hand to catch the second ball. DON'T.

If it is THROW, THROW, DROP, DROP, either
- Keep trying, or
- Go back to Lesson One, or
- Go on to another chapter.

Next . . . can you guess? Yes, eyes closed. If you keep dropping them, begin to peep and see where they've gone. Too far, too short, forward or back? Don't move your catching hand, but do Lesson One over and over again. Improve your throwing!

Lesson Three:
Three Balls

This is it. Take two balls in your best hand, one in the other. No. 1 is at the top of the first hand, with 3 behind. 2 is in the other. Try THROW THROW THROW CATCH CATCH again. That's easy enough. Now, what about no. 3?

Next time, when 2 comes in to land, clear the runway—that is, toss 3 up somewhere—anywhere at first, but eventually *under* 2 and back into the other hand.

There, you've done it. Now, next time, try clearing the runway every time a ball is coming in to land. Try for more successful catches each time, until you can do six regularly. Then go back and check your style. It's bound to be terrible!

Problem
Solving

Unable to get past about 5 throws

Answer: Repeat just 5 throws until that's easy enough. Then start by counting down 5 - 4 - 3 - 2 - 1 - GO! So you start with number 6.

Balls tending to fly forward

Answer: Work against a brick wall. It ruins your fingernails if you keep throwing forward. Or, Walk backwards while juggling.

One arm always in front of the other.

Answer: You don't believe the balls can pass in the same vertical plane. Have faith—and face the wall.

One hand moving a lot—going up to catch, maybe

Answer: Bad throwing. Go back to Lesson One, concentrating on your worst hand.

So now you can juggle. You're in the same club as Serge Ignatov, who can keep 10 rings in the air simultaneously, Paul Cinquevalli, who juggled three 18-kilogram cannonballs, and Kris Kremo, who does 3 pirouettes while his cigar boxes stay in the air.

You're also in the same club as thousands, maybe millions of people who have discovered juggling as a hobby. Some do it to impress people, others to relate to cosmic vibrations, others to make friends and share experiences. When I was in San Francisco, I heard that Saturday mornings were jugglers' gatherings at Golden Gate Park. As I wandered through the park, I approached the crest of a small hill. Ahead of me, the horizon was filled with balls, rings and clubs, buzzing about, intermingling like flies over a pond. Walking on a bit further, I saw the people—a layer of people beneath the layer of flying things. There were about sixty of them, young and old; black, brown and white; rich and poor. I was immediately made welcome, offered the loan of a set of balls, and began to learn and teach, and make friends.

Later, I found how it all started. One juggler needed a partner. He hung posters offering lessons to any potential apprentice/partner. The park was his rendezvous. The first day, too many people came, so he arranged another session. The next week even more. So it grew and grew, and for all I know, it is growing still.

What to Juggle?

I always teach with Bean Bags. They are easier to catch and harder to lose. (When you drop them, they *stay* there). They also rattle, and before long, you've got your own rhythm section.

Cut out 4 panels. Machine sew them inside out, leaving a 1″ gap in one seam. Turn the ball inside out and fill with small, dry, heavy beans, using a funnel. Then sew up the gap strongly by hand. Make a set of 3 balls, the same size and weight. Important hints:

- Use very strong material that won't fray.
- If in doubt use two thicknesses.
- Use 2 contrasting colors for adjoining panels.
- Get the 8-panel look with striped material.

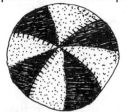

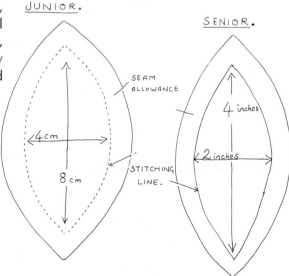

When you've mastered bean bags, move to balls. Heavy rubber balls are best—lacrosse balls, or 2½″ diameter dog balls. You will be able to juggle any ball, from ping-pong to footballs, but smallish, heavy balls are best. The weight of them makes it easier to control the direction, and the catching hand closes snugly around each ball as it lands. You can also use tennis balls, apples, oranges, rolled-up socks, soup cans—almost anything.

Later, I'll go to explain about rings and clubs, but first . . .

A Catalogue of Tricks and Variations

Basic Cascade   You have this one.

Reverse Cascade   The ball passes OVER the one in the air, and down the middle. Try first with one ball, then two, then all of them.

Half-Reverse Cascade   Throw OVER, with the right hand and UNDER with the left. You'll have a shower pattern with a kink in the bottom line.

Cascade to Shower   From half-reverse cascade, send 2 up in quick succession, then shower.

Under Wrist   To do this, the throwing hand goes under the other, and lobs the ball back to the center.

Under Leg   To send it in any fancy direction —behind the back, or sliding off the head —throw the previous ball higher to give yourself time. There are many routes around your body; we'll explore them with one-ball juggling later.

Grab   Catch a ball overhand, twist, and toss up as usual. Try "grabbing" 2, then 3, finally using both hands.

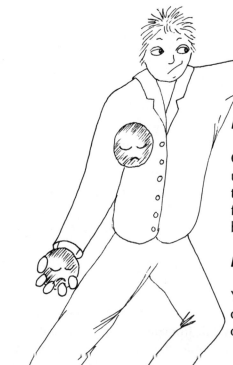

Rogue Ball

One personalized ball begins to "show-off,"—go under the others, under the wrist, and so on. You have to grab it, to bring it back, This is a really good sequence for young audiences, who identify with the "naughty" ball.

Bounces

You can bounce all 3 balls off the floor, either on cascade or shower pattern, or bounce just 1 or 2 balls off the floor during a sequence.

Hideaways	While juggling, put a ball under your chin, or your head, or down your trousers, either bringing it immediately back into the pattern, with the other hand, or stopping to puzzle about it.
Plaiting the Pigtail	This is a "special" which requires some preparation. The effect is well worth it. Attach ribbons or soft rope, 3' long, to your 3 juggling balls. Connect the other 3 ends to one point, like a rubber ring. Your partner holds the ring and, as you cascade you plait a perfect pigtail! Juggling becomes harder as the ropes get shorter, so, when you're ready, simply switch to reverse cascade, and the pattern unravels itself.

Two-Ball Juggling

From one hand, there are at least five different patterns for juggling 2 balls. You should practice them all, with either hand.

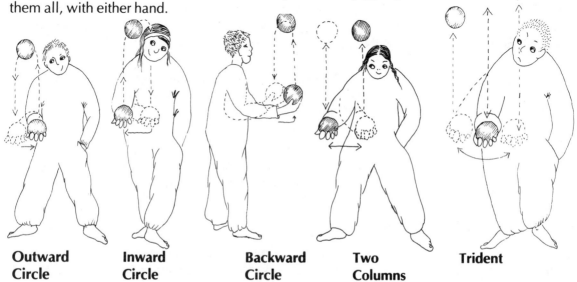

Outward Circle	**Inward Circle**	**Backward Circle**	**Two Columns**	**Trident**

Ball 1 goes up and down center. Ball 2 swings under and goes up alternate sides — i.e., you throw center, left, center, right, center, left, etc.

Four-Ball Juggling

Do the two-ball outer circle with both hands, either in unison or, for better effect and less crowding, alternate hands.

One-Ball Juggling

This is a very pleasant exercise, with a fascination all of its own. It's best to use a heavy ball for this. The basic pattern is a sideways figure 8 across the front of your body (∞ which, significantly, means "infinity").

Swing the ball up from the right hand, across center, so it falls to the left, and gently curve it back up and across, and catch it from above with the right hand. This routine depends on ingenious variations, such as

1. Pass ball OVER other hand before grabbing it from above.
2. Roll it over other knuckles, or bounce it off forearm before catching.
3. Pass ball under opposite leg.
4. Behind small of back.
5. Behind back and up over opposite shoulder.
6. Behind back and up over same shoulder.
7. Short circuit — bounce it off palm of one hand back over the throwing hand,

Apart from 7, the essential motion of this move is *slowing*. Do not jerk the ball back upwards, but "persuade" it.

Five Ball Juggling (and 7, 9, 11!)

This is based on the 3-ball cascade. Begin with 3 in right hand, 2 in the left. Throw alternately from right, left, right, left, right. The problem is that you cannot judge exactly when to throw the next ball as you can with the 3-ball cascade. 5-ball juggling is advanced. But you can do it if you IMPROVE YOUR THROWING!

Clubs

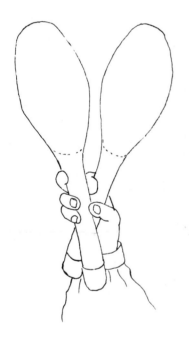

Juggling clubs should be light and well-balanced. Ours are made from children's plastic skittles, with ½" dowelling handles.

Club juggling follows the same pattern as the 3-ball cascade, except that each club makes a complete turn toward you before you catch it (by the upper part of the handle, near the center). Practice first with one, then two.

Here are some common faults:
- Club turns too much, caused by holding the very end of the club.
- Second club too far forward, because you don't believe there's room for two big clubs to cross in front of your little body. Have faith.
- Club flying too high! It should all happen below eye level.

There are many excellent books on juggling, to help you go further with club juggling — or, better still, find a juggler.

Rings

These should be approximately 2" wide, with 12" outside diameter. Cut them from ¼" plywood, and bind them with plastic tape. Cascade them like 3 balls, keeping them vertical. They can go higher than eye-level, and, as they fly slower, many people find them easier than clubs or balls. Certainly, once you've mastered a clean flight, with no risk of them touching, you must try the 5-ring cascade.

Scarves

Cascade 3 chiffon squares, or cotton handkerchiefs. Put them up in the center, and let them float down the outside. It's exactly like the 3-ball pattern, but while balls are *pushed* up, scarves have to be *pulled,*

Working with a Partner

Pair or group work gives you infinite scope for drama, comedy, and downright flash! Here are some suggestions, but from here on you're good enough to introduce your own ideas.

3-Ball Sharing	Stand close to your partner, your left arm around him/her. Your right hand and her left cascade 3 balls in the usual way. Siamese juggling!
The Snatch	Very important for comic routines. As your partner juggles the 3-ball cascade, you snatch no. 1 at the highest point from her right hand, WITH YOUR RIGHT HAND. She keeps juggling. You immediately snatch the next with your left, and finally, throwing ball no. 1 into the air, you snatch ball no. 3 and you have them all. Partner is left juggling with nothing — until she snatches them back.
	Try snatching also from the side, and from above (as your partner kneels).
Perpetual Juggling	As you snatch one from her right, then another from her left, she astounds you and everybody by continuing to juggle 3 balls. Secret: she had 5 identical balls, and was holding 2 out of sight with her smaller fingers, while juggling 3. It's a very easy and natural move to bring balls no. 4 and 5 into this pattern.
Substitution	As she juggles, you snatch a ball from the top of the throw, wait for one throw, then substitute a different ball from below up between her hands. She has to cooperate by doing a blank throw in between — but no one will notice. This is great for clowns, who gradually substitute rolled-up socks for the artiste's glittering balls, or an orange in place of the apple he is eating.

Everything you can learn with balls, you should try with clubs and rings and other objects. Looking through the pages of "Jugglers' World," it seems that there's nothing new to be done in juggling. William J. Fallon has juggled clubs at 18,000' in Nepal. Michael Lauziere has "joggled" 1500 meters in five minutes. Paul Cinquevalli lobbed a 60 lb. cannonball from both feet, to land on his head, in 1909! And in 1981, Anthony Gatto perfected the 4-ball juggle simultaneously with a one-ball head bounce — at the age of 8.

But if what you achieve is new to you, then it's fun. If it's also new to your backyard audience, then it's show biz!

STILTS

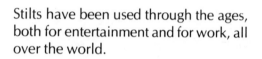

Stilts have been used through the ages, both for entertainment and for work, all over the world.

There's a famous painting by Goya of a village fete, showing stilts tied to the walkers' waists and thighs, as well as ankles and feet!

In Sweden, window cleaners wear stilts. In Les Landes, France, shepherds wear stilts to see further over the flat plains. I have seen "plasterer's stilts" in the U.S.A. made of aluminum, with flexible feet. Hop-stringers in England and Germany are said to wear stilts up to 15 feet high!

The highest recorded stilts mastered were 21 feet high, worn by Harry Sloan in Great Yarmouth, England. The highest worn by any members of my Suitcase Circus were 7 feet, by Paul Quiletti of Craigmillor, Scotland. I tried them once, but found them terrifying, and was very happy to get back to my own little 2'6" pair.

I think everyone, at some stage, has tried to walk on stilts. But almost certainly they were "hold-on" stilts, where you stand on a ledge of wood, hold the top of the stilts, and shuffle along, "same arm, same leg." When you lose your balance, you simply jump down to the ground.

There's a role for these stilts in your circus, just as there's a role for "tin can" stilts, but they are both curtain raisers for the real thing — tie-on stilts.

The advantages of tie-on stilts are:

- Your hands are free for other things.
- You can walk normally, swinging your arms.
- You can wear trousers, or a skirt.
- You can hop, run and dance.

There are disadvantages too:

- If you fall, you can't jump off. You may hurt yourself. You'll need help getting up again.

46

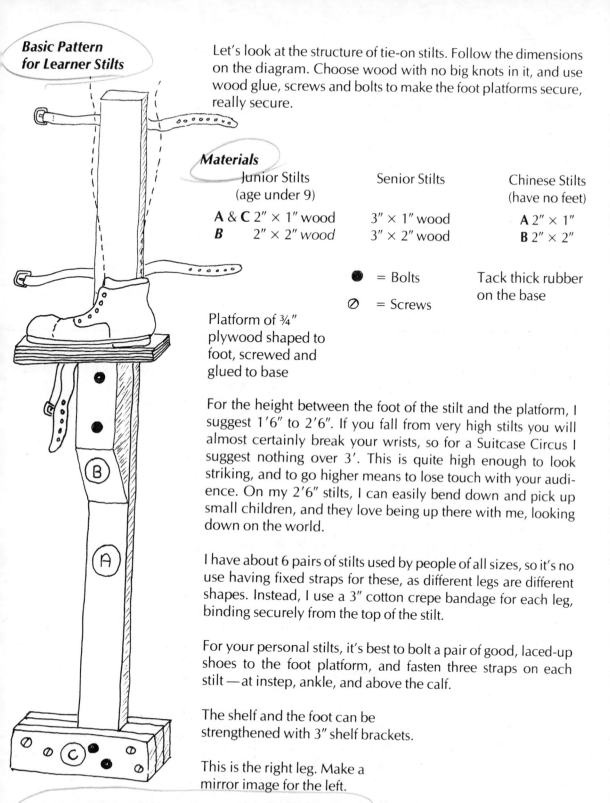

Let's look at the structure of tie-on stilts. Follow the dimensions on the diagram. Choose wood with no big knots in it, and use wood glue, screws and bolts to make the foot platforms secure, really secure.

Materials

	Junior Stilts (age under 9)	Senior Stilts	Chinese Stilts (have no feet)
A & C	2" × 1" wood	3" × 1" wood	**A** 2" × 1"
B	2" × 2" wood	3" × 2" wood	**B** 2" × 2"

● = Bolts

⊘ = Screws

Tack thick rubber on the base

Platform of ¾" plywood shaped to foot, screwed and glued to base

For the height between the foot of the stilt and the platform, I suggest 1'6" to 2'6". If you fall from very high stilts you will almost certainly break your wrists, so for a Suitcase Circus I suggest nothing over 3'. This is quite high enough to look striking, and to go higher means to lose touch with your audience. On my 2'6" stilts, I can easily bend down and pick up small children, and they love being up there with me, looking down on the world.

I have about 6 pairs of stilts used by people of all sizes, so it's no use having fixed straps for these, as different legs are different shapes. Instead, I use a 3" cotton crepe bandage for each leg, binding securely from the top of the stilt.

For your personal stilts, it's best to bolt a pair of good, laced-up shoes to the foot platform, and fasten three straps on each stilt — at instep, ankle, and above the calf.

The shelf and the foot can be strengthened with 3" shelf brackets.

This is the right leg. Make a mirror image for the left.

How to Teach Beginners, Using Footed, Tie-on Stilts

Getting on the Stilts. The beginner sits on a chair, or table, or piano, so he can comfortably put his legs vertically on the stilts. The stilt top goes on the *outside* of the leg. Bind the stilts to the leg with a 3" wide crepe bandage, beginning at the top, leaving an 8" end. Spiral down the leg, binding above the calf, the ankle, the instep, close to the stilt, the heel, then back up again, and tie a bow at the top. This must be done well, as there's a real danger of it working loose.

Standing. When both legs are firmly bound, tight but not painful, stand in front of him, holding his hands, and invite him to move away from the seat. He'll be a bit shaky, and the stilts will feel heavy. Teach him the "safe" position, which is not really very safe — but safer: crouch like a skier, with hands on knees. This gives stability up top, lowers the center of gravity, and means that if he is going to fall, he's half-way there.

Falling. He must learn how to fall. Falling from stilts is never pleasant, and he must learn *not* to fall, but if he does, remember: hands and knees all land together, to share the weight. Tell him if he falls backward to twist, and land forward.

Walking. Walk backwards, watching the beginner carefully, ready to hold his hands. Once he can walk, the problem is, how to stop! Don't let him try to stop dead in his tracks, but instead to take shorter steps, and lift his body weight back up, above the legs.

Exercises

Have someone stand beside you during these, as there's still a chance you may fall. Holding hands with another stilt walker makes you both more stable.

1. Knees up. Get used to taking your weight on one leg, by lifting the other knee, with the stilt hanging vertically.
2. Lift leg out to the side and back again. Be sure to bring it right back to its original place, or you'll gradually do the split.
3. Fold your leg back, bringing the stilt up behind you. Mind your head — and other people's! Practice these with alternate legs.
4. Jump with both legs together. You'll be lucky to clear an inch, but the importance of this exercise is to find your balance again, after landing.
5. Step up and down a low step — 3" to 6". *Down* is particularly difficult in footed stilts. To avoid toppling forward, you should first swivel 90° and step down sideways.

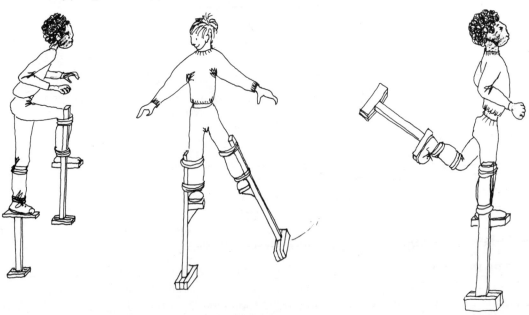

Now you are probably ready to go on to "Chinese Stilts," which have no feet. This means that you can't stand still, but have to shuffle from foot to foot occasionally, just as you would if you were to stand on your heels. Try it!

Why Chinese stilts? For the answer, ask an experienced stilt-walker to go back to footed stilts. It's exactly like the difference between a bicycle, and a heavy, awkward, but more stable, tricycle.

Chinese stilts are *safer* than footed stilts on rough ground. On footed stilts, you can lose your balance by stepping on a match stick! As the stilt's foot see-saws over tiny obstructions, you react as if you're toppling, and may well lose your balance in the other direction. On Chinese stilts, you know that you're continually in an unstable state, so you walk to adjust.

The Chinese stilts are also better on slopes. With big wooden feet, set at right angles to the legs, you can only survive an upward slope by walking on the toes, and then go downhill on the heels. This is precarious. On Chinese stilts, the stump serves as both toe and heel.

Also, Chinese stilts are lighter, and much better suited to running and dancing.

When to Go Back to Footed Stilts

1. For standing still, in a stage play, for instance, where the noise and visual disruption of a shuffling giant would be out of place.
2. In large pantomime animals, like the Giraffe or Elephant, where again, the beast must be able to stand *still*.
3. In playing stilt football (soccer), where big feet are particularly useful for stopping, and controlling, the ball. This game is always a great favorite at our circus festivals. The rules are simple:
    - Each team consists of 3 players and 1 "picker-upper."
    - The playing field is approximately 60' × 30'.
    - The goals are like indoor soccer goals — 10' × 3'.
    - The audience surrounds the field (except the goals) and serves as a wall to keep the ball in play.
    - The referee — in clown costume — announces the lengths of each half. In the interest of fun and entertainment, he may change the rules with the consent of both team captains.

A Dance Medley on Stilts

We usually put the stilt walkers on first, for a variety of reasons:
- Quite often, the Circus has just done a street parade, and while other groups are preparing props, the stilt walkers are ready for action.
- If the performers are in another act as well, it's quicker to come *off* stilts than go *on* them.
- It's difficult to hide stilt-walkers 8 or 9 feet tall, so we may as well declare them as our opening feature.
- They usually need a clear ring, without mats.

Our most common routine for stilt-walkers is a Dance medley. This should be performed to loud music, either live or on tape, with a good, loud percussion accompaniment.

Entry of the Gladiators

4 stilt-walkers march in, arms swinging, knees lifting high. They form a line facing audience. They are followed by a military-style inspector — either a stilt sergeant, or a very small clown. "Halt! three paces forward . . . MARCH! Three paces backward . . . MARCH! SALUTE!"

Waltz

"Take your partners for the long-legged waltz!" Pairs of stilt-walkers (and pairs of clowns, monkeys, etc.) whirl around the ring, the ladies holding their great skirts delicately in one hand.

Swan Lake

"Ladies and Gentlemen, now for the cultural part of the programme, the well-known ballet by Tschaikovski . . . *Stork Lake!*" A line of stilt walkers step gracefully sideways to their left, undulating arms to the right. Then all curve their arms gracefully above their heads, fingertips touching, and pirouette in dainty circles. Finally, they work in pairs, the boys supporting the girls by the waist and arms as they form beautiful arabesques on one leg, the other leg raised horizontally behind them

Rock 'n Roll

The spell is broken by a loud, gutsy tune, and the stilt-dancers break up for free-range stomping, pogoing and twisting.

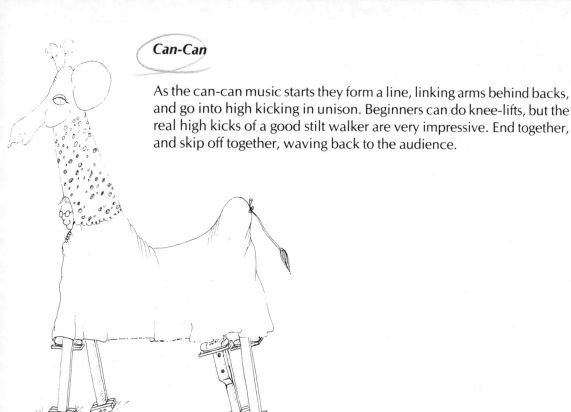

Can-Can

As the can-can music starts they form a line, linking arms behind backs, and go into high kicking in unison. Beginners can do knee-lifts, but the real high kicks of a good stilt walker are very impressive. End together, and skip off together, waving back to the audience.

Other Stilt Activities

Ring Door. (See page 83). Two stilt walkers make a "ring door" by holding the pole supporting a curtain. Or both can wear "Giant" costumes — sack-shaped dresses, 6' wide and 7' long. With arms extended, their costumes make a ring door.

Trapeze Bar. Two stilt walkers hold a pole on their shoulders for a small trapezist.

Head-Stand. A good stilt walker can fall forward onto hands and knees, and go forward into a head-stand, legs spread. This looks very impressive . . . even more so when an acrobat does a dive-roll through the V of the long legs.

Hopping. When you're really confident on your two legs, try hopping. Lift the spare leg gradually higher *behind* you, until eventually you can put your hand back *over* your shoulder and hold the stilt in the air. This gives the impression of a very flexible leg.

Getting up. If a stiltwalker falls, accidentally or on purpose, this is how you should pick him up. *Don't* hold his arms, chest, or waist. Instead, he comes to a kneeling position, and you lift his knees, or upper stilts. As he supports himself by holding your shoulders, he's upright again in no time.

Alternatively, he gets himself up with a poke, again from the kneeling position. Holding high on the pole, he places it vertically just in front of his knees, and pulls. He lifts his right knee high to get the stilt vertical, then reaches higher, heaves, and gets the other stilt up. This is a difficult move, but very effective in a routine using poles as extended arms, just as the stilts are extended legs.

51

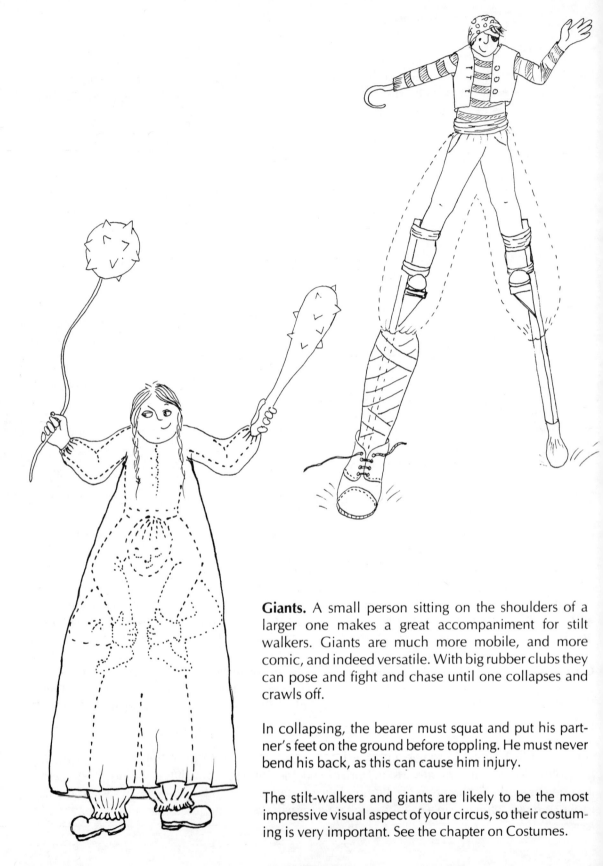

Giants. A small person sitting on the shoulders of a larger one makes a great accompaniment for stilt walkers. Giants are much more mobile, and more comic, and indeed versatile. With big rubber clubs they can pose and fight and chase until one collapses and crawls off.

In collapsing, the bearer must squat and put his partner's feet on the ground before toppling. He must never bend his back, as this can cause him injury.

The stilt-walkers and giants are likely to be the most impressive visual aspect of your circus, so their costuming is very important. See the chapter on Costumes.

CLOWNS

"It is forbidden to do a representation of a clown."
Salvador Dali

"A clown is a poet, who is also an orangutan."
Steve Linsner

Sometimes people say to me, "I'm no good at anything, so I'll be a clown." This makes me so mad! I explain that, to me, a clown must be either brilliantly funny in his very nature, or must be so good a performer that he can afford to be funny about it. As an example, I describe the tight rope performer. He *knows* he can so it. He does it every day. Yet the act is presented in such a way that we all think he is going beyond the frontiers of human possibility. But the clown is different. He gets on the wire — or slack rope — and he does something really clever. He seems to stay on that rope *accidentally!* Given the same apparatus as the high-wire walker, he goes beyond the incredible to achieve the unthinkable, the pathetic and the hilarious.

Clowning is not just a question of dressing up in funny clothes and falling over. In fact, no one should pretend to be a clown. You're either a clown or you're not, and every group of adults or kids will have at least one person who is obviously a clown.

In the Suitcase Circus, there are possibilities for at least five types of clown:

The Grotesque	This is the traditional red-nose and/or big feet and/or baldy head type of clown. In costume or make up, you exaggerate one or more aspects of his body or face.
The Skilled Clown	Unlike the "performer", who makes his act look as difficult as possible, even though it may be easy, the "skilled clown" does the same act, but makes it look easy. He goes to sleep on a slack wire, juggles three balls "because they're too hot to hold," or does human juggling as part of a cops and robbers chase.
The Sad Clown	The most familiar "character" clown. (Another is the American-type tramp clown, with ragged clothes and unshaven face). The white-faced sad clown, however, is a type stretching back to the earliest days of the circus and pantomime. He/she is often dressed completely in white (Pierrot), and is very thin and gawky, doesn't speak, and is the butt of the other clowns' more gentle jokes. Pierrot is too fragile for custard pies or water buckets, but is often good for a comic love scene, in which he doesn't get the girl.
Wandering Clown	You've probably seen him in the big top, with a puppet or a balloon or a small animal, climbing among the audience, giving them an opportunity of close-up contact with the performers. He is very important in the Suitcase Circus, where it's often a very wise precaution to have someone patrolling the audience to watch out for mischief, or to keep the crowd from coming in too close. The clown for this job should be someone with a strong enough personality to be noticed and listened

to, and yet not so bossy as to annoy the kids nor so vulnerable as to stimulate them to aggression. A modest crowd-monitor is what is needed, and one who can entertain at the same time.

The Clown Troupe

Take a dozen of your smaller kids, with red noses, white ruffs, and outsize shoes. The red noses can be made with ping-pong balls, painted red, with adhesive tape around the cut edge to stop it cutting the child's nose. Hold it on with a piece of elastic. A good ruff can be made with a strip of material (about 5 feet long, 6 inches wide) gathered with running stitches along one edge. Any large shoes will do, the larger the better. Shoe paint will make them look even more ridiculous. With a bit of organization you have a clown troupe. Make one of them the leader. Give them all names (Sausage, Custard, Chips, Eggs, etc.) Their role is to fill the stage between the other acts, with a take-off of what's gone before, or a short burst of completely pointless activity— dusting the circus ring or something like that.

Even a group of 5 and 6 year olds can be relied on to do the following:

Clown Tight-Rope

Use a plank of wood, with thick rope nailed along each edge, supported either on chairs, ladders or stalwart backs, at eye-level for most of the audience, so they see only the rope. The kids then traipse along it, doing pretend wobbles, cavorting on their big feet. It's important to get the clowns to put one foot in front of the other, as feet side by side on a supposed tight-rope spoils the effect.

Clown Acrobats

A dozen tumbling toddlers need no organization. Just tell them to keep rolling over each other.

Clown Strong Men

They show their muscles, do push-ups, then suddenly beat each other to a pulp.

Clown Balancing Act

One clown is sufficient for this. He carries a pole with a tray of cups or glasses "balanced" on the top. When his attention is distracted, his stick leans over —but nothing falls off!!! (It's amazing what you can do with screws and glue!)

Clown Animal Act

A parade of toddlers each with teddy bears on the end of a leash will delight the crowd. The bears will obey orders like "Sit" and "Stay" (surprise surprise). They'll even jump through a hoop (provided the clown climbs through first and pulls the lead).

It's good if the Ringmaster gets hopping mad at all these clown "interruptions." Either they sneak on when he's not looking, or else he lets them on for one more chance to prove good. Inevitably the act ends with the ringmaster chasing the troupe right round the ring and off.

Finally, you may attempt a clown act which is carefully rehearsed, and as much a non-stop, complete entertainment as the other acts. Choose the clowns carefully. Help them develop clown characters. But most of all, your clowns must be themselves.

My wife Annie Stainer (a famous solo mime artist) and I and our son Joe (then three years old) were greatly honored to win the Gold Cup (professional class) at the National Clown Picnic in the U.S.A. in 1975. We did it, as we do all our clown work, by being ourselves — only more so. I am short and stocky; Annie is taller and very thin; Joe is just a boy.

To declare that we are a clown family, we all wear the same green and white striped shirts, the same large check trousers, the same red noses, and the same bald wigs. We don't wear make-up. (I have a pet theory: "the more make-up, the less clown," but don't quote me!)

I enter and introduce the strongest lady in the world, "My Wife!" I am the only one blind to the fact that she is about as strong as a day-old chicken. She struts and poses (just to please me), showing off her "muscles," and glowering at someone in the crowd who dares to laugh at her. (Everyone is laughing.)

"She has the sinews of Sampson, the girth of Goliath, the muscle of Popeye . . . and now she will lift a weight of no less than 600 kilograms!"

She suddenly "sees" the (invisible) weight on the stage, and her spirits visibly drop. Nevertheless, to please her husband, she gets her hands round the bar, and grunts and heaves it up, as I, with total confidence in my wife, encourage her with many a "heave-ho." "She's done it!" I turn to the audience. "What a woman!" Etc.

Meanwhile, Annie's upward lift has continued and she's leaning perilously over backwards. She calls for "Joe!" He runs on stage, pushes her back upright, and I call for more applause. As I turn away, it happens again, and again Joe pushes her up. I'm still making the best of it, keeping this applause going, but getting visibly embarrassed. The third time, I step in, and take the barbell from her, only to stumble to the ground under the weight, with the bar across my chest, unable to move. Annie is petrified in the corner, but little Joe walks on, picks up the "weights" with one hand, throws them into the audience and walks off!

A similar thing happens with the juggling. I announce that I'm going to save the show by doing an acrobatic dance routine with Joe. While I'm smartening myself up, Annie, unknown to me, takes little Joe to the side of the stage and returns with a life-sized Joe doll, dressed just the same, which I take, speak to, and tuck down the front of my trousers.

Annie joins me in the dance routine, which is set to taped music, and meticulously choreographed. It includes dance parodies, "accidents," and some impressive acrobatics made to look very casual. Throughout the dance, I'm getting more and more outrageous with the things I'm doing to "Joey."

"Look, I can stand on my head." "Look, Joe can stand on his head!" (As I hold his feet.) "Look, I can stand on Joe's head!"

But the joke's on me, as everyone but me knows it's a substitute. Finally, on the last note of the music, I throw Joe through a paper hoop. Annie catches him up and storms offstage, and I'm left alone, and rather ridiculous.

Not the sort of routine you might expect, perhaps, but one which we've performed with great success in 16 countries, from Puerto Rico to Japan.

My advice would be:
- Choose your specialty clowns carefully.
- Design their appearance with care.
- Make each clown personal, as an extension of their own characters.
- *Don't* do something the audience would expect.
- Weave the plot around a very real event. (In our case it was *performing*. It could be something as real as having a lunch break or sweeping the ring.
- Rehearse it meticulously, so that it can be performed with total confidence.

THE UNICYCLE

The unicycle is an obsession with me, and with thousands of people all over the world.

In Japan, Israeli Jack Halpern started the Japan Unicycle Club from nothing, and he now has thousands of members. He is making plans for a World Unicycle Federation.

In Sweden, Goran Lundstrom, an engineering educationalist, is also a crazy man. He's written a unicycle manual—imports and sells odd-sports equipment—and holds the world record for the biggest wheeled uni, 63" in diameter. (It helps that he is well over 6' tall).

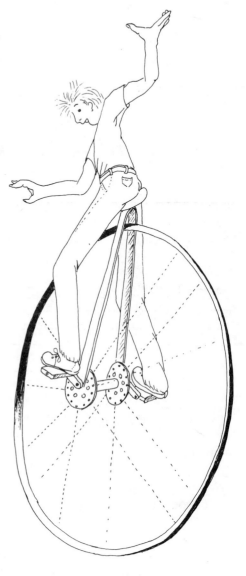

From Surinam comes Sem Abrahams, the undisputed world champion unicycle rider. He won the Unicycle Society of America's Freestyle Category three times before the age of 19. Sem simply has an overdeveloped sense of balance; he can't fall off things. He also has a remarkable father, Carlos, an agricultural engineer who is at present designing a uni for Sem 300 feet (yes, 100 yards) high.

In Great Britain, Brian Davis was the first man to unicycle across the country from Lands' End to John o' Groats. He did it in 17 days—on my very own 28" wheel uni.

As with most things, the U.S.A. is the home of the most dedicated and inventive unicyclists—like Steve McPeak, who rode from Chicago to Las Vegas mostly on a 13' uni (as a sideline, Steve does things like stilt-walking up an inclined tightrope)—like the late Bill Jenack, who taught thousands of people, including blind people, to ride—like Frank Malk, who has designed and rides a motorized unicycle—like the Reverend James Moran of Geauga County, Ohio, the one-wheeled parson.

How is it possible for grown men to become totally obsessed with ways of getting on and staying on one wheel? What is the attraction of the unicycle, which turns adults into kids, and enables kids to outdo adults?

I believe it is the simplicity of the thing. It is such a basic piece of apparatus—one wheel, two pedals and a saddle—which is obviously impossible to ride! It is such a thrill to do the impossible. It is equally thrilling to me to teach others to do it themselves.

Very few people have learned unicycling from a book. Like walking, it's something you just have to learn yourself; and, like bicycling, once learned, it's never forgotten. However, as it took me a month to teach myself to ride a unicycle, and now takes me a day to teach someone else, here are some important hints for beginners:

- Make sure your uni fits you. The most important dimension is your leg length. When you are astride the saddle, your foot should rest on the lower pedal with your leg fully extended.

- Begin on solid ground. Avoid grass, carpets, and bumps.

- You will drop the uni many times while learning, so tape the front and back of the saddle to protect it.

- Don't give up. Aim to achieve a little more each day.

Mounting

Stand near a wall on your right. Hold the front of the saddle with your left hand, with the uni in front of you. "Sit" on the saddle, with the right foot on the pedal at the 5 o'clock position.

Leaning lightly on the wall, "stand" on your right pedal. The uni will roll back, and you lift your left foot onto the left pedal, and pull it back until the pedals are horizontal.

You may not think it, but this is the stable position! Keep your right hand on the wall, extend your left hand for balance, and pedal forward. Always move forward to the next horizontal pedal position. Vertical pedals mean trouble!

Catching the Uni

Before you launch off into space, get used to falling off correctly, because you've got hundreds of falls ahead of you.

Stand in the starting position, right foot a 5 o'clock, but off the wall. Hold saddle front with left hand, and step on right pedal. You'll probably sail right over the saddle, and as it shoots out behind you, CATCH the back of the saddle with the right hand, and simply land on your feet.

I've had the pleasure of teaching hundreds of people to ride, but the sound of a unicycle crashing to the ground still makes me cringe. Please learn to catch it, and save yourself and your saddle.

Later, when you're performing, you should master the rear dismount. With one foot extended downwards, stand on it and step back on the other, holding the saddle in front.

"Lift-off"

When you feel ready to leave the wall, find two friends, and rest your hands on them, on either side, and have them walk with you. Don't lean heavily, but try to find your balance. Remember to keep your weight on the saddle, and use your feet to move the wheel to a point below your body weight.

My son Joe was 7 when we had the pleasure of meeting Sem Abrahams at a Spring Festival in Tel Aviv. Sem was then 19, and a very modest and brilliant young man. He took over the job of teaching Joe to ride his 16" wheel Miyata, and introduced me to a new teaching technique, particularly good for young children. He stood *behind* Joe, and put his hands forward for Joe to rest his hands on. This gave Joe the chance to choose his own speed, and direction, with moveable parallel bars travelling with him.

Once you have mastered the basic techniques of riding the unicycle, it's time to move up through the increasingly difficult and unlikely things that you can do on one. I'll list them in the order that I learned them, and then the things I've yet to learn. But I won't tell you where I stand on the list!

Standing Mount. Mount as described above, but without holding anything. You'll need to do the half-pedal backwards, then push off on the right foot.

Walking, or Running Mount. Walk with the uni in your right hand in front of you. As the right pedal comes up toward you, step on it and jump up onto the saddle and push forward on the left pedal. The trick is to press the right foot down *only enough to stop the uni,* not to pull it backwards.

Stop/Start. As you ride along, stop momentarily by stepping on back and front pedals together. When you feel you're about to fall, lean forward and pedal off again. This is a preparation for rocking and riding backwards.

Riding Backwards. Learn this early, by stop/starting. Then stop, back pedal, and start again. Gradually increase the number of back pedals.

Side Mount, Forward. Hold the uni in your right hand, beside you, left foot on the pedal. Swing the right foot up and over the saddle, down to the right pedal. Make a half back pedal, then off on the left foot.

Side Mount, Backwards. Hold the uni on your right, this time holding the front of the saddle. Again put your left foot on the left pedal, then swing the right leg backwards over the saddle to the right pedal.

"Suicide" Mount. Hold the uni in front of you, pedals horizontal. Balance the uni, let it go, then jump up on it. You MUST get your feet on both pedals simultaneously, or it's very painful.

Rocking. Stop/start, and include one back pedal. Get into a rhythm of one back, one front; then make the movement smaller and smaller until one leg stays almost extended, and the other lightly touches the upper pedal.

When you're good enough, you'll be able to release the upper pedal momentarily to flourish the foot forward, or, eventually, to kick 6 cups, 6 saucers, spoon and a sugar lump up onto your head, like Rudi Horn of Germany. The important thing to realize when rocking is that your body remains in the same place in space, and the uni moves back and forward beneath you.

The Giraffe Unicycle

It is easier to make a high unicycle, and, theoretically, it's easier to ride one. You can make one from an old bicycle, with certain adjustments. This diagram shows how:

Clearly you'll need some engineering skills, to cut, weld, and braze the metal, but many a father has made such a unicycle for his son. It would make an excellent school metalwork project.

A smaller, chainless unicycle is harder, because you need to replace the hub with an axle for the pedals, and bearings capable of taking a great strain.

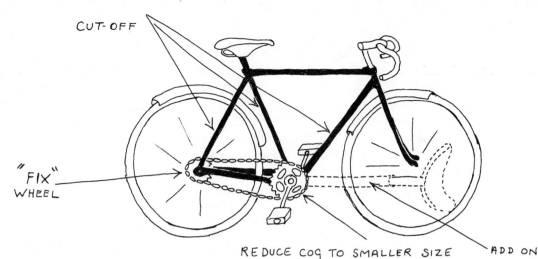

CUT-OFF

"FIX" WHEEL

REDUCE COG TO SMALLER SIZE   ADD ON

But why is the "giraffe" easier to ride? For an answer, get a friend to balance a pencil on his finger tip, while you balance a broomstick. You'll find the broom easier to balance because, as it leans, you have ample time to adjust the position of the bottom and to regain balance. Whereas your friend will find that when the pencil falls, it just falls!

So, on the high bike, you've got much more time to adjust your wheel position. But, as I'm sure Sem Abrahams would admit, if he ever sits astride his unicycle 300 feet above Manhattan, there is an extra factor which spoils the simple physics of the thing. FEAR.

However, on your 4', 5' or 6' high giraffe, you need not worry. Your feet are never more than four feet from the ground, and you should always be able to land on your feet, preferably in front of the uni, with your hands holding the saddle.

But the question you'll be asking is, "How do you get on it in the first place?" Here are three methods:

The Gilly Gilchrist Lamp-post Mount

- Stand the uni against a post or door jamb, left pedal forward.
- Stand on top of wheel with right foot, while holding saddle firmly against post/wall.
- Put left foot on front pedal (pushing uni against wall) and swing up onto the saddle.
- Now with both feet on horizontal pedals, you can turn, and ride away.

Monkey Mount (for quick, agile climbers)

- Hold uni by saddle, with it leaning slightly forward, left pedal *vertically* down.
- Step on wheel with right foot.
- Then, nimbly, put left foot on pedal. As uni comes upright, it will move slightly backwards.
- Swing right leg over. Sit on saddle and pedal away.

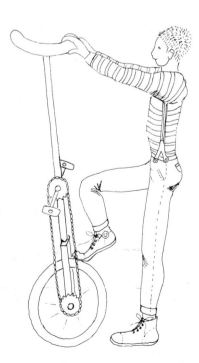

Running Mount

In Jack Halpern's comprehensive list of skills, the running mount on the high uni is graded as super advanced. In my experience, it can by learned very easily, by anyone who is well coordinated—and bold.

You need to take your courage, and the saddle, in both hands. Approach the mount like a sort of crazy pole vault. But the pole vaulter has a light pole, a hole in the ground, a bar to go over, and foam rubber to land on. You have an unwieldy machine to push along. You have no hole, but must stop the charge by standing on the brake. This would easily push you backwards, but no, you must sail up in the air. Then, you must land, not on your feet on foam rubber, but on your softest part, on a hard seat, 6 feet up, and start pedalling. It hardly seems possible!

Let's break down the process:

- Hold the saddle with both hands, wheel out front.
- Push it till the right pedal is coming up towards you.
- Step on it (right foot) and step high with left foot, as uni goes up vertical.
- Step over the saddle, place left foot on pedal, sit, release hands, and go!

Routines

Now, you have learned unicycling as a sport, and with your friends you can race, play tag, basketball, and obstacle races. But, for your circus, you need some routines.

Ultimately, you'll work out your own, but as an example, I'll detail a unicycle routine I've done before, with six riders, lasting abut 10 minutes.

- All six unicyclists enter, one after the other, fast, and circle the ring clockwise. Joe, being smallest, comes in last.
- Riders change pace and go into twos, hand on the other's shoulder. Still circling, they move closer to the center. Inner riders extend and join right hands, and the team spins as a 3-spoked wheel. One pair break away, separate, and each joins the end of the row, making a big, sweeping line.
- Three go off, leaving a group of three, with little Joe in the middle, all still circling, and holding each other. Joe suddenly drops his uni, but, supported by the others, he continues pedalling through the air!
- These three go off. Two of the others come back, holding hands and waltzing, tangoing, spinning around each other in the dance of the unis. Finish with bow, and exit.
- One rider speeds in with Joe sitting on his shoulders. Both have arms outstretched.
- Two run in with long rope. A third rides in and starts skipping as the others slowly turn the rope. (This "pogo-ring" is done by holding the saddle tight, and jumping. The pull on the saddle and the bounce in the tire keeps you going. After a while you needn't hold the saddle. (Once I saw Sem Abrahams pogoing in a slow circle, while juggling three clubs).

- These three take applause and leave. Joe runs in and sets up a line of bottles (or bean bags) and the others speed in and slalom in between the obstacles, finally stopping to pick up one each off the ground.
- One performer rocks on the spot, catches three balls thrown by another, and juggles.
- Two come in with giraffe unicycles, and demonstrate the monkey mount and running mount (with drum rolls and a couple of failed attempts).
- They ride along with linked arms. I chase behind with Joe on my shoulders. I go through, under the arms, but I've lost Joe. He's hanging on their arms like a monkey!
- Someone brings in a set of broad, shallow steps, with a ramp on the other side. One rider circles around, approaches the ramp, thinks better of it, circles again, then rides up ramp and straight down the steps! (This is done by pogoing alongside the step, and springing up and on to each step. When he reaches the top, he rocks, then rolls down).

- I clear the steps away, then feign tiredness and lie down, center of the ring, and put a 6' x 1'6'' ramp across my stomach as a blanket. One by one, the riders ride over me, see-saw fashion, finishing with Joe, the littlest. As I get up, they circle, come to a straight line, dismount to rear, and we all take a bow, and run off, carrying plank and unis.

I often include other wheeled vehicles if I'm performing indoors—a baby in a stroller, and skaters and skate boards being towed by the unicyclists. It all adds up to a very exciting spectacle.

STRONG MEN

They need not necessarily be strong; need not be men. In fact, it's funny to have a "strong man" act with a tiny little girl. However, it's sometimes useful to include this act in your circus when you have some older boys to involve, who have nothing to offer but their size.

The basic costume is to have the boys strip to the waist, and roll their jeans up to mid-calf. Then, if there's time, paint blue "tattoos" like anchors and snakes on their arms, black hairs on their chests, moustaches and fierce eyebrows. They should take up and maintain statuesque poses, with that earnest self-absorption that characterizes the Mr. America type.

I'll describe a routine which, in itself, is TOO LONG, but it will include enough ideas for you to choose from. It'll be a mixture of joke acts, and some which demand real strength and coordination.

Entry	Stirring music, and a steady bass beat, as the squad of strong men parade in, showing their biceps. Little Emma is conspicuously smaller than the rest. They take up positions in the ring, and at a given signal begin earnest old-fashioned exercises, like knee-bends, and push ups.
	All together, the men stand and take up posing again. Little Emma is flat out on the ground, exhausted.
Wrestling Match	A stage hand runs out with a wrestling ring (a band of 1½" wide white elastic). Four volunteers hold the corners, to make an instant wrestling ring. One of the strong men, as emcee, announces a wrestling match in the flamboyant style we've all seen on T.V. Two of the men swagger into the ring, and go into a rehearsed wrestling match, full of trips, grabs, spins and groans, just like on T.V., ending with the loser tied up in the elastic ring.
A Real Act	One of your bigger boys takes a *real* phone book, shows it to the audience, and, then, with a mighty fanfare and drum roll from the band, *tears it in half*.
	This needs considerable strength, but there's a secret to it, which I'll tell if you're interested enough to write to me.
Fake Weight Lifting	Whatever other clown books say, DON'T make weights with a stick and a black balloon at each end. It looks silly. Take more care. Cut out 1" thick styrofoam discs (with a hot knife) the size of weights, and fix them to a wooden or plastic bar. Spray the whole lot black or blue. Just be careful that the paint won't dissolve the styrofoam.
	One by one the strong men attempt the lift, and collapse exhausted. One finally does it, but falls with the bar across his neck. Little Emma runs on, picks it up, and runs off with it — chased by the others.

In this situation, ALWAYS run at least once round the ring before exiting.

Juggling Cannon Balls

A very impressive routine, with a terrifying ending. This, too, has a secret, but I'll reveal it as it's my own. I advise you to do it only if you're a good juggler, strong, and quick-footed.

I swagger on, posing. Behind me, Little Emma drags on a very heavy bag. From it, she manages to lift, only just, a 20 lb. cannon ball. At least the audience, even if they handle it, are prepared to accept that it weighs 20 lbs. In fact, it's an 8 lb. 13 oz. shot, from a sports shop. This she rolls across the floor to me.

"First, Ladies and Gentlemen, I shall juggle with this 20 lb. cannon ball. You'll notice that my feet are protected only by the softest of shoes!" One-ball juggling (see p. 00) is quite easy with the cannon ball, but be careful not to knock yourself out if you do the pass upwards behind your back, and over your head.

"And now, Emma, another!" She heaves another out, and rolls it over to me. If I'm indoors, and have my 1½" diameter rigid plastic gas-pipe ring, she rolls it along against the inside of the paper. Its momentum carries it slowly round the ring to me, with a very satisfactory rumbling sound echoing through the floor. Alternatively, she gives it to someone in the front row, and it's passed hand to hand to where I'm waiting on the other side.

"And now, Ladies and Gentlemen, two-cannon-ball juggling!" I clang them against each other once or twice, then "OUCH!" I suck my little finger, glaring at the audience, who laugh. Then after a couple of "throw, throw, catch, catch," I go into the two-ball shower, ending with a high throw.

"Any more, Emma?" Yes, there's another, which she begins to hand round, "No, just bring it over." She does, although it's clearly a struggle, and gives it to me. Now I *really* juggle them. It's not easy to start, as each hand is full of one, and you have to hold the third between them, and lob it up the middle to get started, Ending is even harder. Either I let the last one drop — and risk smashing the floor — or do a high throw, pass a ball from the right to join the other in the left hand, then catch with the right.

I take applause, then begin to roll the balls back to Emma. After rolling one, I decide to do something else. "Ladies and Gentlemen, I'll now juggle *two* 20 lb. cannon balls in one hand!"

I perform this — and it's getting more difficult all the time.

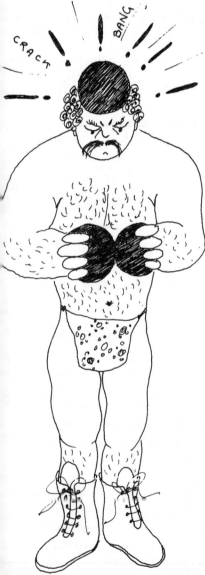

"Finally, Ladies and Gentlemen, a trick performed by my late Grandfather. Bring that ball back please, Emma." She does. As I take it from her, I say, "Take my hat off, please, Emma, and I'd like everyone in the audience to take their hats off as a mark of respect to my old Granddad, who died performing this act. Silence please."

Solemn drum roll, then I begin to juggle the three balls, one, two, three, four, five, six, then SEVEN goes high in the air and as it plummets down, I fix my eyes on it and move forward. It lands incredibly smack on my forehead. It bounces off, I catch it, and, staggering slightly, take my bows and leave the ring. Emma follows me with the bag which, to the discerning eye, looks suspiciously heavy.

The secret? A simple substitution. Do you recall I gave the third ball back to Emma briefly? Well, when she brought it back for the finale, it was an identical ball, but instead of cast iron, this one was black plastic (I got it from a toy ten-pin bowling set, and taped over the 3 holes).

Even so, the act is difficult. You have to juggle two balls weighing over 8 pounds, and another less than 8 ounces. Also, of course, if you head the wrong one, you're dead!

You may feel, as I do when it's a young audience, that you have to show it's a trick, so they don't go home and knock their brains out. For this, I put the three balls down after the trick, Emma looks at them, lifts up one heavy one, then the other, and finally the light one, which shoots up in the air. She bounces it on the ground, calls me a cheat, and chases me off.

Kung Fu

A lovely comedy sequence, in which the bigger lads can throw themselves around to their hearts' content, and not hurt anyone. Choose the smallest boy or girl you've got, and introduce him/her as the Kung Fu champion of the world. She stands at the center of the stage facing a line-up of the big lads. One by one, these "challengers" hurl themselves toward her, fists up, and screaming bloody murder. She deftly sidesteps each one, and with a back hander of a kick, throws them behind her on an ever-increasing heap of groaning bodies. This must be rehearsed, of course, and it's essential that the "champ" knows which side of her the attacker will run. They should pass her on alternate sides, left-right, left-right, so she knows which way to step and where to kick. She ends by putting one foot on the pile, and holding her arms high in victory.

Human Trampoline

You need a strong stomach, and preferably a big one. Lie on your back across the mat, knees up, feet firm. Next to you stands a catcher, his back to you, hands in the air. The flier uses you, literally, as a springboard, jumping on you with both feet, between the ribs and the groin. As he approaches, you tense your stomach, which absorbs his weight, and spring him upward by pushing with stomach and legs. He must bunch himself in the air, take the catcher's hands, and land standing on the catcher's shoulders. (The flier MUST be light. You MUST be strong. Be ready to roll out of the way if the flier slips back from the catcher's shoulders.)

Inverted Pyramid

Just like the acrobats, the strong-men can end with a pyramid, but theirs is inverted, You can design your own shape, but don't go more than two-high without qualified supervision.

As more and more people climb onto your base man, they must go up symmetrically — one on each side.

Like so many circus acts, it needs *presentation*. If you just climb up and then come down again, it's nothing. The presenter should use phrases like "Never before in the history of the children's circus . . ." and "He will lift 6 men, which is a total of 620 pounds, or an equivalent of 9,920 ounces of lead!"

WRESTLING

A stagehand runs out into the ring with the band of 1½" wide elastic. Four volunteers hold the corners for the instant wrestling ring. "Ladies and Gentlemen, we are proud to introduce the smallest wrestlers in the world. Their names are 'Egg' and 'Bacon.' They'll need plenty of support, so let's have everyone on this side of the ring shouting for Egg. Egg . . . Egg . . . Egg! That's good. Now, over on this side. let's hear it for Bacon . . . Bacon . . . Bacon! Now, for the contestants."

The Ring Door bursts open and the midgets hurl themselves into the ring, already in a tight clinch. As the Ringmaster lifts the elastic and guides them in, we see that Bacon is definitely bigger than Egg, but Egg is lighter on his toes. Their arms are clasped tight, each around the other's shoulders, and we can only see the back of their heads as they heave and twist, grunt, groan, and roll over and over.

Bacon lifts Egg high into the air, carries him to the "ropes" and drops him clear over the edge. But plucky little Egg holds on, climbs up, stands on the rope, bounces three times, and leaps straight onto Bacon's chest, throwing him to the ground, never once releasing his grip.

So the bout goes on, with the little fighters inflicting horrible blows on each other, and the referee — always with their feet!

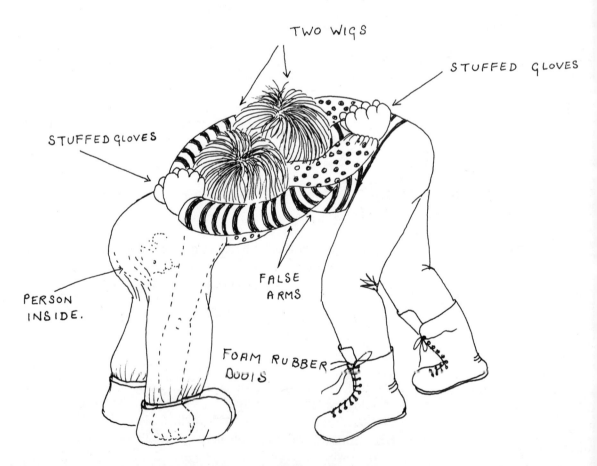

TWO WIGS

STUFFED GLOVES

STUFFED GLOVES

PERSON INSIDE.

FALSE ARMS

FOAM RUBBER BOOTS

68

Optional Ending No. 1	The time-keeper rings the bell. "End of round one!" The wrestlers fall exhausted, face down on the ground, still in a clinch. Referee: "Break it up, boys, back to your corners." No move. "Break!" Nothing.
	Referee kneels down, looking concerned. "What's the matter, boys?" Bacon (or Egg): "I'm stuck!" Referee calls stage hands to carry them off by their feet, and calls for a round of applause for "those brave little fighters, Egg and Bacon."
Optional Ending No. 2	The timekeeper rings the bell. "End of round one!" The fighters stop. Bacon straightens his legs, and slowly little Egg rises in the air until he seems to be in a handstand above Bacon. For the first time, the audience sees the underside of the fighters. Egg's feet rub against each other. His little boots drop off, to reveal —*hands!* These hands reach into Bacon's belt, untuck Egg, and remove him, like a sweater, revealing the face of the exhausted but talented performer, the "One-Man Wrestlers."
	This will win a round of applause for the performer, who bows, picks up the boots and costume, and leaves the ring.

The picture shows how the suit is designed. It is important that the "Egg," or smaller half, be made with bulky material, or be padded to hide the contours of the real head and arms. Egg's boots should be made in such a way to enable the performer to work comfortably on his knuckles. Finally, to help the illusion, give each wrestler a color scheme for his trousers, back, arms, and maybe even a cap.

Hints to the performer to perfect the illusion:

- Avoid showing your underside, where you'll have holes for eyes and mouth which the audience shouldn't see.

- Remember that Egg must stand on the ground just as firmly as Bacon. So don't let your hands hang in the air, and lift them only one at a   time.

- Keep your head down, or it'll look as if Egg's got a football in his pants.

- Move each character separately. In other words, take care not to synchronize arm and leg movements.

- Give each one a voice —a high one for Egg, a low one for Bacon. Each should cry out when he is attacked.

This act originates in China. When Jo Hignett, the illustrator of *Circus in a Suitcase,* was in China recently, she saw it performed by street buskers. She observed a refinement in the costume which made the whole thing much more comfortable. The little men each wore a *skirt.* This meant that the performer didin't need his head inside Egg's trousers, as the heavy skirt hung almost to the ground. Then, to take his applause and collect his money, he simply stood up, and the skirt hung downwards from his chest.

HOOPS

Browse around any playground or toyshop; think over all the "crazes" of the past few years, and you'll see the makings of an act. Hula Hoops are a good example.

Hula Hooping. Beside the obvious hooping around the neck and waist, try lying on your back and spin four hoops—one on each limb.

Diving Through. Clowns, acrobats or dare-devils can all use the basic technique of a dive forward roll through a hoop. To paper the hoop, first glue together enough tissue paper to fill the circle. Then put impact glue on the hoop itself, and lay it on the paper; then trim off the excess.

Rolling Hoops. Throw a hoop away from you across the floor, at the same time spinning it back towards yourself. As its forward motion fails, it will roll back.

With three hoops you can juggle horizontally. You can flick them into the air, jump over them, or try leaping through them at the moment they change direction.

ROLLER BOARD

This is also known as the Rola-Bola, and consists basically of a board and a cylinder. The cylinder should be strong and smooth, of approximately 5" diameter by 1' long. We use either wood or heavy-duty plastic pipe.

The act consists of standing with one foot on each end of the board, which is placed across the cylinder. As the cylinder rolls from side to side on a hard surface, you have to keep your balance on the board.

FIRST, place the cylinder, end on, a foot from a wall. Lay the board across the cylinder and step on the lower end.

NEXT, supporting yourself by your hands on the wall, put your other foot on the upper end. As you put weight on the upper foot, the board will roll away from that foot.

NOW, keep your balance. You'll find that as you shift weight rhythmically from foot to foot, the board will take up a regular side to side undulating movement. The secret, as you'll find out on the slack rope, is to keep your trunk and upper body in the same place, while from the waist down you move from side to side.

WHAT NEXT? To make an act, you must do more than this. So either:
- Juggle on a Roller Board.) wi scarves
- Handstand on a Roller Board (difficult unless you are a first-rate skateboarder).
- Roller-Board atop a table. This looks risky, but is safe pro vided that the table top is no shorter than the board itself.
- A Roller-Board "Dance." Two or more of your company move in step, with simultaneous stop/starts, and even jump/ turns (jumping in the air, turning 180° to land and continue).

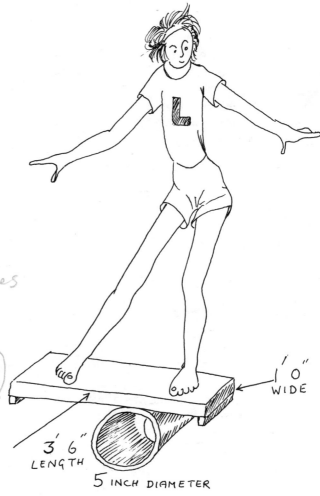

1' 0" WIDE

3' 6" LENGTH

5 INCH DIAMETER

DANGER. Be careful when beginning. It's harder than it looks, and the board can easily roll away beneath your feet, and you could land heavily on wrist or hip.

When I was a student at the Ecole Nationale du Cirque in Paris, there was a student who had a ladder strapped to the wall. He started the first day on one single roller board. Next day he brought a second cylinder. He put the first parallel with the wall, and the second *across* the first, topped with the board. He hung on the ladder and stepped gently onto this infinitely wobbly combination. After two days, he brought in a new cylinder — and a new board. By the end of two weeks, hanging from the eighth rung of the ladder, he launched himself successfully on the incredible combination of (from the bottom): one cylinder, a second cylinder across it, a first board, a third cylinder UPRIGHT, a second board, a fourth cylinder across it, and finally — a third board. INCREDIBLE!

Later, I saw him juggle 5 ping-pong balls, in a shower, from his mouth! He was aiming to do this on his rola-bola pyramid!

BALANCING ACTS

As I've explained in the Unicycle chapter, it is easier to balance a high object on your finger than a low one. It is even easier if there's a relatively heavy object at the top. The sword is easiest to balance by the tip, and a broomstick by the handle.

I simply offer this observation, and invite you, especially the clowns, to use it in your show. Balance your hat, a tray of drinks, or a bucket of water high above the heads of the terrified audience. Walk a tightrope or see-saw, still balancing the object. Toss the object across to your partner.

Be sure that your audience can see that you're not faking it, by either beginning or ending with the objects at ground level, and separated.

In most good circuses, especially those from Russia and China, the pole-balancing or "perch" is a specialty act performed by a troupe who have been training for years, with custom-built equipment, using fail-safe harnesses. At the Circus World Championship, I saw the Sarach Troupe from Russia perform an unbelievable sequence. Two men on the ground hoisted another on 20' long poles. He in turn had a 20' pole on his shoulders. At the very top, inches from the flapping canvas of the big top, the girl in the troupe, having climbed up those poles, went from a handstand to a crab, on a tiny platform. Then, gripping the apparatus in her teeth, she lifted her legs and arms, to hold the incredibly difficult Marinelli position.

The true difficulty of this act was proved when a gust of wind blew the canvas in on her. She slipped and fell from the pole, and all the poles fell apart. All the parts and all the artists were left dangling in the air, to be lowered to the ground by the Ring Boys.

THE TIGHTROPE

For many people, nothing personifies the sheer magic of the Big Top more than the tightrope walker, circled by the spotlight, in a world of her own, high above the ring.

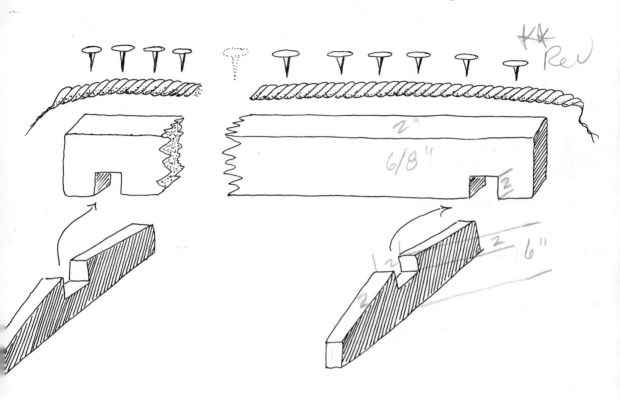

All children picture the high-wire artiste from below, defying gravity by balancing on a thread. They are often very diasppointed to find, at the Suitcase Circus school, that our practice tightropes, illustrated above, are only 1'6" and 2'6" high.

Even in performance, I recommend that your tightrope should not be more than 6' high, as there is a real danger of broken limbs or wire burns if you fall off.

The tightrope (or tight-wire, to be more accurate), is not an easy thing to rig, and its installation should be supervised by an engineer. Use ½" or ¾" diameter steel wire, attached at each end to the floor or walls, with the straight stretch supported on two A-frames or tripods. A turnbuckle is integrated at one end to achieve the necessary tension.

For an indoor rig, unless there are custom-made plates attached to the floor or walls, it is necessary to screw through the floor-boards deeply into the joists, to attach the ends of the wire. There are many variations, such as a block and tackle instead of the turnbuckle, and a platform built over or under the wire at each end.

To walk the wire, you should wear soft-soled shoes. The sole must protect your feet from the cheese-cutter effect of the wire (ouch!), yet be supple enough for you to feel the wire clearly and shape your foot around it.

Beginners will often try all sorts of ways to keep their feet on the wire, by walking pigeon-toed or splay footed, or even by standing sideways with both feet facing the same way! There is only one correct position, and that is to have the wire from your big toe to your heel.

This brings us to the second principle of wire walking: *stand on one foot at a time*. The other foot helps you balance by just touching the wire, or by being held in the air, but your body weight is on one foot. It has to be, to enable you to walk along.

To keep their balance on the high wire, the immortal funambulists like Blodin and Karl Wallenda used balancing poles up to 40' long. You do not need to; in fact you could not! The principle of a balancing pole is that the ends are so low as to bring your center of gravity *below the wire*. On our low wire, the pole would touch the ground. Beside, the pole weighs up to 30 pounds, and is only a help to the experienced —and strong —wire-walker.

What you need is advice:

- In the stark words of Karl Wallenda: "On the wire is your life; below is your death." In other words, however low your practice wire may be, stay on it!

- Keep your body upright; do not fold at the hips. Use the arms, well above your sholder level, to balance.

- Look forward and see the wire extended before you. Do not watch your feet.

- To help you balance, use a small umbrella, or a fan, which *pushes* the air. Once you have grasped the principle of which way to push, you will find it a great aid.

For a performance in the street or park, you may not have a wire, but you can still perform your act — on the *pole.*

Two men (it could be two stable stilt-walkers) hold the pole on their shoulders. The performer either rises up with the pole, swings up, or steps across from a shoulder stand. Her act is simple, but special. She walks forwards and backwards, she turns, she juggles, she steps through a hoop. If she is good, and spotters are standing by, she may walk the pole blindfolded. (Remember, it is easier to see through a black blindfold than a white one). Finally, if your wire walker is one of those brilliant young girls on the gymnastic beam, you may go on to all the variations of the traditional pole act. (Strangely, it is the people of Poland who seem to feature most often in the Pole act, just as they traditionally win the Pole vault event at the Olympics. It seems that, where Poles are concerned, you have to be Polish to shine!)

In the Circus pole act, the girl on the bar performs most of the moves you would expect on trampoline, which the difference being that the 2" × 8' springboard is held up by two strong men, whose job it is to see that it always placed where her feet or bottom are about to land.

Even if your balancing girl cannot finish with a back somersault from the pole, she can still end with a flourish. In our show, one of the men lifts the bar gently from his shoulder and bends to put it at his feet. The girl steps down the 45° angled pole, puts both hands on his bent back, springs into a hand stand, to short-arm press, and lands gracefully on her feet to take her applause.

The slack-rope is essentially a comic device. It is a good one for the Suitcase Circus, as almost any thick rough-spun rope will do, and it can be slung at almost any height and angle between hooks, trees, columns, or even cars.

Oleg Popov, the great Russian clown, is the master of many skills, including the slack rope. He wanders on to it, as if by accident, and panics, only staying up there by dint of crazy antics with his walking stick. Finally, it is all too much for him. He takes his jacket off, lays down under it, and falls asleep —*on the slack rope!*

As on the tightrope, the technique depends on standing on one foot at a time. As on the roller board, you should isolate the top of your body, which stays still, while your trunk and legs relax and enjoy the wildly oscillating movement of the rope. Because of this isolation of the top half, juggling on the slack rope is not difficult.

ESCAPOLOGY

I have a copy of a British magic magazine, with a center page spread, featuring a picture of a huge and deadly bonfire of cardboard boxes, piled high on a beach, burning merrily. The caption reads:

The Great Bonfire Escape

The outside stunt by Eric Ward at the International Brotherhood's annual convention of magicians at Hastings really set the pace for a sizzling convention.

The photograph shows the intense flames of the inferno. Eric was nailed inside a wooden box in the center, and was still there for about another minute after this picture was taken. This built up a fantastic suspense as you can imagine.

After what seemed like ages and with the huge crowd's nerves on edge, Eric burst from the center like a rocket to take the tumultuous applause from the crowd that packed the promenade.

After a short spell in hospital, Eric has now completely recovered and is back in show business.

Good old Eric! I have a soft spot for Escapologists, who always seem to have to work harder for their living than anyone else in the business.

It is not my intention to be giving away other people's secrets. So I will give you one hint, and divulge only two methods.

1. If you are escaping from chains, use lots and lots and lots of chains.

2. Houdini's Nerve. Harry Houdini, the all-time great escaper and illusionist was superbly strong and agile. He could withstand great pain; he could dislocate his shoulders. He had great self-control. He never panicked, and could consciously relax his body and mind to survive without oxygen for incredible lengths at a time. But he was also very clever. Many books have been written explaining his tricks. The one that impressed me most was the brick wall escape.

He is alone on stage. The stage has been inspected by a committee. There are no secret tunnels, no curtains, no mirrors. A gang of bricklayers comes on stage and begins to build a wall around him. It completely encircles him. The last the audience sees is his impeccable white-gloved hand waving over the top of the solid ring of brick.

When he is completely immured, the gang crosses over to the other side of the stage and builds another, identical ring of bricks. When this one is finished, they wait. Everyone waits. The audience looks from one wall to another. Suddenly a sound is heard—from the second ring of bricks. After a few minutes of chipping and scraping, enough bricks collapse for Houdini to clamber out of the *second* ring of bricks! He is still immaculately dressed.

How did he do it? The answer is laughably simple. With all eyes on Houdini and the wall, who's going to count the number of bricklayers in a gang? A spare overall covering his evening dress was all he needed to stroll across the stage with the others, in full view of the audience!

3. The Pickle Family Circus-in-a-Suitcase. I would not give this one away if I hadn't used it myself on several occasions. In my version, my wife, Annie, has finally driven me to distraction. I bind and gag her and put her in a sack. I drop the sack in a big basket. I lock the basket, strap it up, put chains round it, and put padlocks on the chains. Then, to round things off, I bring on a folding screen and unfold it, in front of me, in front of the basket, just long enough for you to read the words, two feet high, THE END.

Then, as I take the screen off again, and fold it up, you realize it isn't me holding the screen. It's Annie! She smiles apologetically at the audience, and seems genuinely surprised to see the big basket jumping about and to hear my muffled voice inside. Naturally it takes her a few minutes to unlock the padlocks, the chains, the straps, the lid, the sack, the ropes and the gag to let me out but it's all worth it for the applause she gets.

How do we do it? Basically, through a huge hole in the back of the basket. The chains and padlocks are very necessary to give Annie time to get out of her ropes and gag, and then again for me to be back in. The crucial moment is when I open that screen, and she has to get out, and me in, quickly and neatly, without too much giveaway sound.

TRAPEZE

Rigging a tightrope is difficult. Rigging a trapeze is either easy or impossible!

The basic equipment is a steel bar, 1½'' in diameter, about 2' long, suspended horizontally by ropes at each end. It should be high enough for the performer to hang from it and not quite touch the ground. The corners should be padded. Rather than explain how we make our trapeze bars, I would urge you *not* to make your own, but to buy them from a gymnastic supply company.

If your ceiling has reliable rafters or beams, then you can hang a trapeze. If not, or if you are outdoors, then you are relying on your two strong men and the pole again. Here are some basic single trapeze movements:

The Hang. Grip the bar over-hand, with thumbs around the bar. Your hands should be as far apart as your shoulders. You may like to use gymnastic chalk on your hands. Personally, I find that the palms of your hands will tell you when your body has had enough, and chalk may deceive you.

The Knee Hang. Swing the legs up, between your hands, resting the back of the knees on the bar. With spotters on either side, or with a safety harness, let go one hand at a time, then hang. Really hang by releasing the contraction of your pelvis, and let your arms hang too.

HORIZONTAL BAR.

Attention. Hold the bar again, and straighten the legs vertically upwards, until you are ''standing at attention,'' upside down.

Bird's Nest. From hanging, swing legs up until the tops of the feet are against the bar. Push the body through, and look up. Come out of it by collapsing backwards through the arms.

Skinning the Cat. From hanging, pull legs up, through the arms, and down the other side, as far as you can bear it. Then go back again.

Angel. Go up as if for a Bird's Nest, then release on hand, and the *opposite* leg. The hanging leg will be supported against the rope. The Angel position is with your front facing down, your head up and spare arm and leg extended.

Catcher's Hang. Hold the *center* of the bar. Swing legs up, straight, and between the ropes. Pull the body up until your pelvis is against the bar. Open your legs, then bend them, so the knees are outside the ropes, and the lower legs parallel and horizontal. You can now let go with your hands, and the weight rests mostly with your thighs on the bar.

Partner work should not be undertaken without an experienced coach, but from this hang you can begin to suspend a partner, either straight, or in a bird's nest, or in another catcher's hang using *you* as a trapeze.

Ankle Hang. This is the one that makes them gasp. You have all seen it. The daring young man on the flying trapeze hanging by his knees reaches the full extent of his swing, way over the audience, and suddenly—his legs straighten out!

Is it a cramp? Is it sucide? Is it disaster? NO. It is knee hang to ankle hang, and it is quite simple.

Do it with a good spotter. In your knee hang, be sure that your legs are all apart, and your feet flexed outwards. As you straighten your legs, the feet fit snugly *outside* the ropes, and you end in a very safe position, with the bar snug against your Achilles' tendon.

Do not do this too late in your practice or your routine, because it is a long way to curl up again, to grasp the bar to come down.

Sitting on the Bar. From a knee hang, grasp the ropes one at a time, and pull yourself up to a sitting position. By all means wave and pose, but keep at least one hand on a rope until you are ready for the

Backward Dismount. This is easier on a static bar—but very effective on a trapeze. From sitting, grasp the bar overhand, either side of your hoops. Straighten up, and slide down until the bar is across your upper buttocks. Then simply roll over backwards, keeping a grip on the bar until your legs are vertical for landing. This takes practice—and needs a spotter.

SAFETY. Always have a crash mat under the trapeze, at least 6″ thick. Always have competent spotters who know what might go wrong. Never improvise. If you get a new idea, talk it over with someone first. If it has never been done before, there is probably a good reason.

COWBOY AND KNIFE-THROWING ACT

The glorious days of the Wild West are inextricably mixed with the development of the American Circus, so it would be sad not to include some sort of Cowboy or Indian theme in your show. I would not encourage children to throw knives at each other, to shoot real guns nor to eat real fire. But here are some ideas:

The Lariat

The circus cowboy's lariat, or lasso, is made from heavy rope, with a small noose at one end. The other end is passed through, and tightened to form a loop about 10" across. Holding the rope to hang down at arms length, you begin to circle the rope across the circumference of the loop. As it turns, and you give it more slack, the loop grows bigger. If you can master this, try one in each hand, or try stepping into the loop and make it move up and down your body. I once did a work-out with a circus cowboy standing on my shoulders (in his high-heel cowboy boots and spurs!) It's the weirdest feeling seeing a horizontal ring of rope, eight feet across, undulating up and down in front of your face.

If you are obviously not going to make it as a Rhinestone Cowboy, you can save the act by sending on the Circus Steer . . . a converted pantomime horse. You could make a hilarious act of catching, roping, and branding the beast!

The Whip

A whip cracks because the tip breaks the sound barrier. So my Physics teacher told me, and who am I to doubt his wisdom? It also breaks the skin of anyone unfortunate enough to make contact at that instant, so be careful.

In the Suitcase Circus, it breaks paper. One performer holds up the daily newspaper, open in front of his face. I step back, crack the whip, and it cuts the paper neatly down the middle. He takes half a sheet, and —CRACK! I do it again. And again, and again, until he has only a tiny piece, 3" square. This he rolls up like a cigarette, and puts in his mouth.

I take careful aim. He says his prayers and CRACK! The whip lashes toward his face. The cigarette flies from his mouth, and he is completely unharmed.

The audience is flabbergasted, and we are pleased that our rehearsals and preparation have worked out. It was quite simple really. First, I have to be sure that from where I stand, the whip never quite reaches his paper, or his face. But the audience can't see that.

Second, we "doctored" to the newspaper by scoring it with a sharp blade, so that an imperceptible tug tears it neatly in half.

"Ladies and Gentlemen, these knives are so sharp that they are almost invisible!" Etc. Of course they *are* invisible. Your skill as comic mime should carry the act. Your partner, too, plays a vital part, as her terrified eyes and twitching limbs show the audience just how close those "knives" are coming, as she stands against the board.

Before throwing your final blade, you should be all bull and confidence as you accept the blindfold and allow yourself to be spun round and round. Nor should you even notice as your assistant grabs the handle of the knife embedded in her stomach, stares unbelievingly up at you, and slumps forward, flat on her face. You simply accept the crowd's laughter as your applause, take a bow, and walk off with dignity, stepping gingerly over your prostrate erstwhile assistant.

The first-aid clowns come and take her away on their stretcher. But that is another act.

FIRE EATING

I am very particular about fire-eating in the Suitcase Circus. Most of what we do is designed to stimulate audiences to try it themselves. But not fire. It is too tempting and too dangerous.

We do perform a fire act occasionally. Some of the older teenagers have been through a careful training of both technique and precautions and we perform it only in special 'theatrical' conditions—not in the back-yard.It worries me when street performers, stinking of inflammable liquids, eat fire and happily blow flames at random over the audience, often ignoring the wind direction.So I will not tell you how it is done. But I will happily give some hints.

1. Fire-eating and fire-juggling rarely works outside in sunlight. It just is not impressive.
2. Beware of the wind.
3. Indoors, beware of curtains and the ceiling, and of spitting on the audience.
4. Never divulge what liquids you are using. I keep mine in a black bottle marked 'Fire Water', with a skull and cross-bones.
5. Do not use petrol—it could blow your head off.
6. Whatever you use—there is a risk of Pneumonia!
7. Do not eat fire if you have dentures—they melt!
8. Have a bucket of water handy.

After all these words of caution, let me say I love to watch fire-eating done well. Like everyone else, I am terribly impressed by performers who walk on hot ashes, put burning coals in their mouths, and who juggle flaming torches. But there is a place for all this—with the professionals.

In all these techniques, I have tried to indicate what I think is reasonable for you to try with your own local group. Naturally, you can go further. The thrill of the Circus is the fact that professional performers are ready to go further—to take risks on our behalf.

However much we value our own and our children's achievements nothing is worth the risk of injury, and the pain and guilt that goes with it. So have fun—but be careful.

HOW TO PUT ON A SHOW

If you've been booked to perform indoors, make sure:
• There's a "dressing-room," or at least, a room to enter from.
• There's head-height for stilts and pyramids.
• The floor's not too slippery.
• You have enough time to set up before the audience arrives.

If it's an outdoor show, be sure:
• There's an indoor hall, in case of rain.
• There is access to toilets, and, if necessary, dressing rooms.
• You have permission for outdoor performance.
• You have power to your sound system.
• You can park your van next to the ring site.
• The site is clear of glass and dirt.
• That your audience knows where you are.

The "Open-Air" Tent

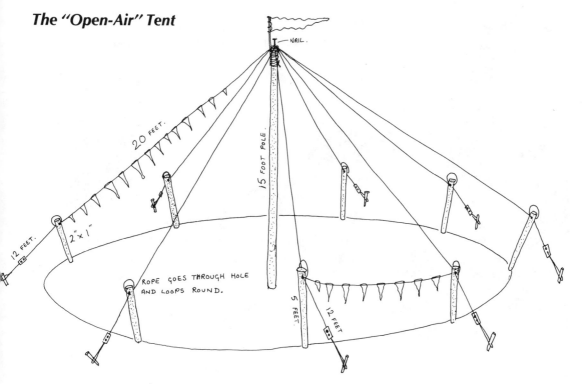

BUNTING CAN BE STRUNG BETWEEN THE FIVE-FOOT POSTS AS WELL AS FROM THE MAIN STAYS.

This consists of a pole 14 feet high — (bamboo, 2 × 2 wood, or an inflexible plastic drainpipe).

The pole, with a nail or ring at the top has 8 rows of bunting radiating out in all 8 directions. Each row is joined by string or rope which is attached to the top of a 5 foot post and down to a tent peg, with a cleat on each, to tighten.

These tent pegs are the only things that stick in the ground, and if you're not on grass, you can attach the lines to fences, cars etc.

If you have enough bunting, you can string it horizontally between the tops of the poles.

This open-air tent looks great from a distance, and once inside, the members of the audience feel very much part of the show.

An extension of this idea is to hang a 6' high 'wall' of canvas or nylon sheeting from the 8 poles. This gives you a large area to paint your banner, or suitable circus pictures, and also contains your tent, so you can charge admission.

Another delightful variation is to suspend a parachute on the radiating spokes of bunting. This makes a good sunshade, and your big top is even more tent-like.

But don't get tempted to join a roof to a wall unless you want to get into the jungle of licensing your 'tent' for theatrical performance.

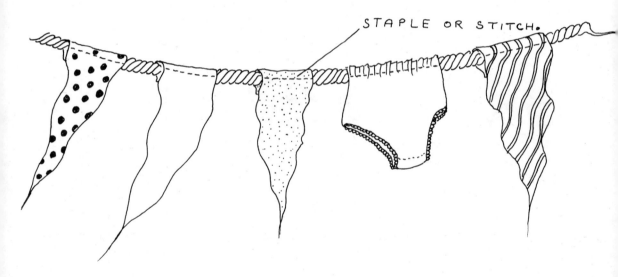

The Ring

The simplest ring is a rope 40 to 60 feet long, knotted end to end and laid on the ground. The audience can pull it out into a circle and sit around it. Even if they're all pulling together, it will retain the shape of a circle. Behind the front row, people can kneel, the next row can sit on chairs, and at the back they can stand. This way 200 people can easily see everything that goes on in the ring 20 feet across.

You can also make a ring with bunting, plastic gas-piping, cardboard cartons, or wooden boxes.

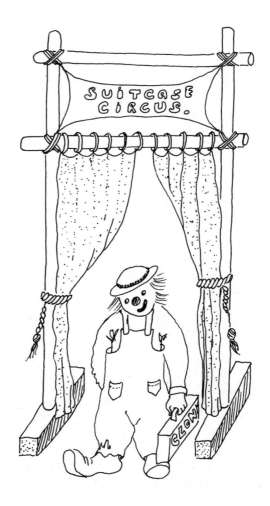

Nothing distracts attention from a circus act more than the sight of the last act dismantling and the next act getting ready. The answer to this is the Ring Door. There are many ways to design this, but basically, you need a curtain, at least 4 feet wide, which will act as a backdrop to the ring, and mask the activity backstage.

An essential job in the Suitcase Circus is that of the curtain holders. Their job is to keep the curtains closed at all times except when people are passing through — into the ring. Exits must be made *around* the curtain.

Do practise erecting and dismantling the tent, before the the big day. Eventually you will find that 4 people can do it in 5 minutes.

In your rehearsals, especially of acrobatic routines, you must bear in mind that there will be a center pole, and if you use mats, these will need to be laid on either side.

The Parade

Having set up the tent and started up some of the circus music (live or tape) you're ready to go off on the PARADE. But leave some competent and responsible people in charge of the tent and props while you're away.

The parade will help the performers get into the mood for the show, and it will also generate excitement in the area. Most important, it will help attract an audience. DON'T go more than half a mile (10 or 12 minutes) and DO plan your route first. Avoid crossing roads if possible, but if you do have to cross them make sure there are adults to stop the traffic.

The main problem with the parade is that the front goes too fast. There are solutions to this. Either put stilt walkers at the front; they can't go very fast, or stop frequently to let the stragglers catch up.

Parade Order

Stilt-walkers (with catcher in front and behind just in case).
Jugglers — only 2 balls each unless they're experts.
Bikes.
Animals — (disciplined real ones or kids in costumes) and their trainers.
Band — drums and kazoos with some good uniforms.
Strongmen.
Tight-rope walkers.
Unicyclists.
Adults looking after stragglers.

Back at the tent have some performers showing the audience to their 'seats,' while the parade of performers circles outside the ring, smiling, clapping, and waving.

Parade Song

A catchy simple song or tune helps a lot. Put the base drummer in the middle so that everyone can hear the beat. Encourage by-standers to join you and clap and sing along.

Ringmaster

Must be a confident and magnetic personality, even if he is the villainous melodramatic type. He must be prepared to focus all the attention on himself in the case of any delay or mishap. It would help if he had a running argument with one particular clown which could be used at any moment for a bit of comic relief.

The Ringmaster must have every act ready to begin and end at his command (or whistle), except for the clowns which will appear as a law unto themselves. In fact the off-stage producer or stage manager is mainly responsible for making sure that one act follows another in quick succession and with maximum energy.

You must rehearse bringing props on stage, e.g. mats, chairs, balancing poles etc., as smoothly as possible. Make each prop 'belong' to someone. This could be the responsibility of a 'props squad' who have no other job, or it can be shared among performers.

The Order

Have plenty of variety of action and let the show come to a good climax. Don't let it get like a boring old school gym display. I suggest something like the following program, which must be prominently displayed backstage.

1. Stilts	6. Wrestlers
2. Apes	7. Hypnotist
3. Unicycles	8. Clowns
4. The Horse	9. Acrobats
5. Jugglers	10. Dare-devils—Pyramid

The Audience

Keep them happy. You don't want their attention wandering from the ring. You could have a "wandering character" in the audience, a good clown ideally, who should be able to spot trouble or boredom in the crowd, fix it and direct attention where it's wanted. Don't leave this to the Ringmaster. He should not have to deal with confrontation.

Avoid performers standing in one place for too long as this will be blocking some of the audience view. The Ringmaster too, should keep on the move.

Any group act should get itself together outside the ring, not in the ring area.

The Ending

End with an exciting act, like a fast moving acrobatic sequence or a record breaker like human juggling or "dead man's leap." The Ringmaster should declare the last act in advance so that the audience is prepared for it. He should use some kind of patter. "Ladies and gentlemen, now for the final act of our show this afternoon." As he joins the applause for the final act he should thank the audience for coming and tell them to let their friends know about the show.

If you want to clear the area of people quickly to facilitate packing up, then have another parade, around the houses so that the children hopefully, will drop away. Naturally you'd leave some of your people at the site to take down the tent and tidy up.

MUSIC

To appreciate the difference music can make to an act, try the following exercise:

1. Acrobat runs up to the mat, does a forward roll, and runs off.
2. Again, but as he rolls, clash a cymbal.
3. Again, but give a drum roll as he runs up, then clash cymbal.
4. Again, but begin with a short fanfare on the kazoo, then drum and cymbal as above.
5. Finally, the whole lot, then as he comes out of the roll, blow a jaunty march like "Entry of the Gladiators" while he runs off.

With this sort of musical treatment, it's difficult for an audience to resist bursting into applause at even the simplest act.

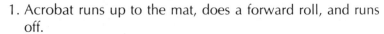

I love to have live music with a circus, but I cannot always get it, and it is not always suitable. Quite often I survive with a recorded sound track, a tape operator and a drummer.

This is not unheard of in the professional circus. Since the heyday of Merle Evans, who led bands up to 36 strong for Ringling Brothers, the financial restraints have steadily increased. Today I have seen several small professional circuses operating with only taped sound and a live drummer or, occasionally, with one of those electric organs that can be played with one finger and sound like the Ringling band in all its glory.

So, you may be forgiven by appearing with a band of 3 kazoos, a tuba and a violin, which may be all you can find.

The special skill of Merle Evans and other circus band leaders is to choose a tune which fits the act, from an Elephant's Rhumba to an Aerialist's Waltz, and to be able to pause, change, and finish tunes in split-second coordination with the act in the ring. This harmony between the music and the performance is hard to achieve with taped music, or a band that plays slowly or only from musical scores.

You can overcome this problem somewhat by having an independent drummer. With drum rolls, cymbal clashes, and other percussive thuds and squeaks, he punctuates the action, topping and tailing each act, highlighting the falls and flourishes, while the band, or tape, rumble away in the background providing atmosphere.

However, if you do have a band of youngsters who can play a combination of instruments more or less in tune, you should time the acts, then choose tunes to suit the action and fill the time, and hope that both end at the same time. It is also useful to learn a few "segues," all-purpose musical phrases which can plug gaps, and lead from one tune to another.

A selection of suitable tunes for different acts:

Parade:	Fucik, *Entry of the Gladiators*
	Sousa, *Hooray for the Red, White and Blue* (or any march)
Acrobats:	Khachaturian, *Sabre Dance*
	Marquina, *Spanish Gypsy Dance*
Trapeze:	Leybourne-Lee, *The Man on the Flying Trapeze* (or any waltz)
Unicycle:	Williams, *Theme from Star Wars*
	Traditional, *Daisy, Daisy*
Wrestlers:	Tchaikovsky, end of *1812 Overture*
Juggling:	Joplin, *The Entertainer*
Stilts:	Medley, including march, waltz, ballet, rock'n roll, can-can

You can make a very presentable clown band from everyday objects for sale in a hardware shop:

Spoons

The traditional cockney rhythm section. Two dessert spoons held between the fingers (either side of the big one), back to back, in such a way that they rest a quarter of an inch apart, but when tapped on the other hand, or the knee, or rattled down the left hand knuckles, give a very satisfying crack!

Washboard

Another rhythm instrument, introduced in the blues era, and revived by skiffle boards in the 50's. Wear thimbles and run them up and down the ribbed face of the board.

Musical Saw

Take a long blade, good-quality saw, and a well resined cello bow. Sit on a firm chair, with the saw handle between the knees, blade up in the air, jagged side facing you. Grasp the top of the blade with you left hand and bend it down to the left, exerting pressure with your thumb to give the blade a slight S-bend.

To make a sound, draw the bow straight upwards across the flat side of the blade. Change the note by exerting more and less pressure with your left hand, and develop a tremolo by jogging your right knee.

The effect, once you get it, is unforgettable—a baleful, haunting wail —not to be used too much, but ideal for a risky act like the tight rope.

Tea Chest Bass

Place the tea chest upside down. Fix a 4' length of string at one corner of the top surface, by inserting it in a hole and tying it to a small piece of wood inside.

Tie the other end of the string to the top end of a 3' broomstick. The bottom end of the broomstick then rests in the middle of the top of the tea chest. Steadying the box with one foot, you pull the stick, tightening the string, and pluck it, like a double-bass. The vibration goes through the string and stick, using the chest as a sound box.

Garden Hose Trumpet	Take a mouth-piece from trumpet or horn, insert it in a length of garden hose, and in the other end insert a household funnel.

If you can play a bugle or trumpet, you can play this, and the effect is terrific. Imagine 20 feet of hose, coiled round and round you like a euphonium, or laid across the laps of the front row, with a small clown at the far end rotating the funnel like a radar dish. If you swing the funnel end round and round as you blast, the effect is much like a police siren.

The main ingredients you need for a Suitcase Circus Band are (1) a musician, and (2) imagination.

COSTUMES

Spangles, sequins, boas and stilettos, jodphurs, jump-suits and gladiator gear. That's what circus is made of.

No one expects your Suitcase Circus to come up to the standards of the Big Top, where a single costume can cost up to $500. But it is worth making an effort. When you put on a show, you are drawing attention to your visual appearance. It should be special. Let's look through the program, and consider the different costumes for each act.

Stilts Walkers

Stilt trousers must be made to measure, from the walker's waist to the stilt's feet. Each leg must be at least 35 inches wider in circumference than the waist. The reason for this is that the trousers have to hang neatly over your real feet. It is also very important to use heavy-duty material, like upholstery fabric, to avoid nasty dents and creases around your own feet.

Remember to put the trousers on *before* the stilts, and roll them up over the thighs while strapping in.

Stilt skirts are also very effective, making the wearer truly statuesque— but beware of high winds! The skirts can be made either with elasticized or wrap-around waists, and should be as full as possible to allow for leg lift.

Make the stilt-walker even taller by giving him a stove-pipe hat, and a snug-fitting waistcoat or jacket.

Acrobats

Girls should wear leotards, and possibly footless tights for more confidence. Normal gym leotards can easily be glamorized with the addition of a few sequins and tassels, at the collar, bust, and hips.

Boys can wear shorts or track-suits.

For a suitable all-around acrobatic costume, try a combination of puffy sleeves and harem pants, all in the same material, worn over shorts and T-shirt, or a leotard.

Jugglers

No particular costume is traditionally required for jugglers or unicyclists, but something loose and colorful should do, or something with a theme, like Spanish or Chinese.

Strong Men

Bare torsos, with hairy chest make-up, jeans rolled up neatly to just below the knees. Big boots. For the real "Tarzan" look, make a one-shoulder leotard with leopard-skin or tiger-skin fabric.

Wire-walker

The wire-walker or rope dancer is something of a ballerina, and girls look good in tights and a tutu, possibly with a coronet or plumed hat.

Ring-Master

The ringmaster is traditionally a horseman, and thus has evolved his blend of evening wear and riding habit. Red coat, black trousers, polished shoes, a black top hat aand white gloves. This is the uniform — but you wear what suits you.

Clown

The white-faced clown, familiar in the clown families of European circuses, has a fascinating history. He is the authoritarian clown, usually accompanied by an "Auguste," a red-nosed, scruffy, unlucky, cheeky fellow. The Auguste suffers every indignity, from custard pies and buckets of water to exploding trousers. But the white-faced clown comes through it all untouched.

His costume is dazzling and elaborate, usually with puffed sleeves and stylized, expansive hips, narrowing to finish below the knee, over white tights and rhinestone shoes. Look carefully, and somewhere you will see in the pattern of his costume some evidence of a diamond or triangular pattern.

He is descended from Harlequin, the flamboyant original clown in the 16th century street theatre, "Commedia dell'Arte." His first recorded costume was covered in patches and tatters, representing a beggar, someone to be laughed at. So he could also be the precursor of the modern-day tramp or hobo clown. But, as the years passed, his patches became formalized, and for a hundred years, his costume was a kaleidescope of red, blue and green triangles, connected by lines of yellow braid. Later, the triangles became diamonds and the braid black, matching his mask. By the 19th century, Pierrot and the fool had become his clowns. He was the boss. He had the best costume, he gave the orders, he never got wet, and he didn't even have to make people laugh. In the 20th century circus, white-faced clowns like Francois Fratellini and Francesco Caroli continue that tradition, and act as a foil for the Augustes and comedians.

The point of this long story is that a clown's costume is often the result of a stylization taken to extremes. Just as the patches of Harlequin's coat became a pattern of diamonds, so big feet became *huge* feet, a drunkard's nose became a red flashlight, and a baggy jacket became a tent!

So, for your individual clown costumes, go to extremes. Have them wear absurdly bright colors, ridiculous long ties, or painfully short trousers.

For your clown troupe, aim at repetition. A family of clowns at the Craigmillar Children's Circus—two brothers and a sister—each wear red, tubular ankle-length dresses, with big sneakers, white ruffs, red noses and bald wigs. The total confusion about "which is which?" adds a great deal to the comic effect.

MAKE-UP

In a theatre, the effect of up to 50 kilowatts of colored lights shining on stage has the effect of highlighting the garish, like costumes, and scenery, and wiping out the subtle, like faces. This is why most actors on stage and T.V. wear make-up. It is to emphasize what is already there.

The principle of circus make-up is the same. Even if you are not performing under lights, you may well decide to wear make-up to highlight your features, and make yourself look special. This, of course, brings in the second reason for make-up. It is the security of a mask. In an earlier chapter I described how the macho lads from Pilton were quite happy to wear make-up when they realized it gave them a group identity, and individual anonymity.

A new generation on make-ups is on the market now. In the past there were only "pancake" makeups in pastel shades (easy to apply, but easy to sweat off or rub off), and "grease-paint" in vivid colored sticks, which were fun to apply, but took ages to get off with greasy cold-cream, often resulting in sore eyes and chapped lips.

The new make-up which I use, Kryolan Aqua-color, comes in pancakes of what seems like grease, but it is water-based. You apply it with a damp sponge, or with any paintbrush. The colors can blend or overlay, and are sweat-resistant. You can even buy a fixative spray. It is said to be non-allergenic, so it's suitable for all children. But make-up is not cheap, and should be used carefully and kept clean and tidy.

Here are simple ideas for performers' make-up:

Girls on the Tightrope, Trapeze, etc.	Eye shadow in silver or gold; eyebrows stylized and extended outwards and up, Cleopatra-style. Rouged cheeks and lipstick. Maybe a sequin, or glitter dust to emphasize the cheek bones.
Jugglers	So that I can tell at a glance, backstage, who are the juggling troupe, I paint colored balls on their cheeks, forehead and chin.
Strongmen and Daredevils	If they are bare-chested, a hairy chest is obligatory! Decorate their arms with ''Popeye'' type tattoos of anchors and snakes. A moustache does wonders for their morale, either a dapper, turned-up Salvador Dali type, or the mean Charles Bronson turned-down look.
Clowns	The white face, made famous by Deburau, the first great Pierrot, evoked laughter in the 19th century because it made the clown look ill, weak, or like a baker covered in flour. The red nose, as worn by Emmet Kelly or W.C. Fields, shows the clown either in the throes of a very bad cold, or extremely drunk. Big feet, big ears, big teeth, all these are handicaps which, when worn by the clown, make us laugh.

So, with the clown, as with the other performers, the make-up exaggerates what is already there. Once you have decided whether the clown is to be a ''White-face,'' a ''Character'' or a ''Grotesque,'' remember the following traditional guidelines.

White-face

The white base should cover the neck and ears, too, and should come as close as possible to the eyes, to avoid the red-ringed look.

You should never copy another clown's make-up, but respect the *style*. The white-face clown has a hard mouth, in an unusual color. The nose is sometimes colored, but often white. One *ear* is often red, and the most unusual features are the eyes. They are *different*. One often has an ornate decoration of arch and swirl, while the other may be barely lined. Sequins and glitter may be added, to match the glory of the costume, hat and shoes.

Character Clown

Oleg Popov wears a minimal make-up. He highlights his eyes and mouth, like any actor, and adds a touch of nose-putty to accentuate his already turned-up nose. Far from being a caricature behind a mask, Popov is essentially himself.

The cinema clowns—Chaplin, Keaton, Laurel and Hardy—have their own natural faces which are totally recognizable and archetypal.

They are character clowns, and support my highly debatable theory: ''The more make-up, the less the clown.''

Emmet Kelly created his Weary Willie character on paper, long before he thought of joining a circus. Kelly was originally a cartoonist, and drew the character for a commercial advertisement. No doubt, he was looking in the mirror at the time, because he only had to fill out his normally thin nose, and accentuate his mournful looks with an unshaven chin, and Weary Willie came to life. You could easily copy Kelly's make-up, with the tired eyebrows, red-rimmed eyes, and turned-down mouth, but before you do, remember Kelly's own cautionary words:

"You can have the best make-up, the craziest costumes and what not, but if you can't act, you are doomed to be just another run-of-the-mill clown. Too many clowns nowadays run out, go through some silly motions, and seem to be saying, 'Look at me! I'm funny! Laugh!' That's a hell of a way to clown!"

The Grotesque

The Auguste, who works with a white-face clown, and other individual Grotesques in the tradition of Lou Jacobs, Coco, and Felix Adler have one thing in common. They use make-up to distort their faces into something quite unnatural, but instantly recognizable as a clown.

To do this, concentrate on the **mouth.** For a big smile, paint extended lips from the bottom lip upwards. For a sad face, take the mouth downwards, in white against black, and add thin lines down from the corners of the real mouth.

Perhaps the most startling mouth make-up is the extra goofy **teeth** that you paint on the lower lip. Outline the teeth in black, extend the lips on either side, and keep your mouth shut! You'll not believe your own reflection in the mirror.

The best red **nose** is made with a ping-pong ball. Cut a rounded oblong to fit your own nose tip and line the edges with plastic tape for comfort. Then paint the lot with red enamel paint. Fasten it either with thin elastic knotted through holes in the side, or with sticky tape inside the ball. The latter method looks better, but will fall off if not applied firmly *before* you add make-up.

Eyes can change their expression by surrounding them with a shape of color. Consider the panda, and you will appreciate that patches converging at the top give a mournful look. Consider Bugs Bunny; eyes and eyebrows extended up onto the forehead give a constantly surprised, jaunty look. Experiment with other shapes.

Wigs can be made by sewing hanks of wool around the edge of the crown of an old felt hat, after you have cut off the brim. For a bald wig, use half an old plastic soccer ball—with or without a fringe of hair.

Collect pictures of circus performers. Draw sketches. Experiment on yourself and each other until you find the make-up that is just for you!

BIBLIOGRAPHY

CIRCUS

Hammarstrom, David Lewis. **Behind the Big Top.** A. S. Barnes & Co., New York, 1980.
A very candid book about the American Circus, seen from backstage, full of information and background details about the sawdust superstars.

Speight, George. **A History of the Circus.** A. S. Barnes & Co., New York, 1980.
A breathtaking piece of research; a book I dip into often, and can never put down. Full of anecdote and amazing detail, and illustrated by hundreds of prints, posters and photographs.

Verrey, Peter. **Here Comes the Circus.** Paddington Press, New York, 1978.
If you could have only one book about the Circus, this one would do. After two chapters of history, the chapter headings read like a Circus program — Horses, Animals, Clowns, etc.

CLOWNING

Crowther, Carol. **Clowns and Clowning.** Macdonald Educational, London, 1978.
A book designed for children, with the usual history of clowning, but embellished by many practical suggestions for would-be clowns, including activities suggested by my good friend, Chris Harris.

Hugill, Beryl. **Bring on the Clowns.** David and Charles, London, 1980.
A coffee-table sized book with an entertaining text and lots of glossy pictures, telling the story of clowns through the ages.

Towsen, John. **Clowns.** Hawthorn, New York, 1976.
Written by a clown who is also a scholar, this thick book won't make you laugh, but will tell you a lot about people who have made the world laugh. An excellent book.

Woodward, Ian. **The Story of Clowns.** Ladybird Books, Loughborough, England, 1976.
From the popular and inexpensive Ladybird series for children comes a really excellent book, which, with a no-nonsense text, and hand-painted illustrations, tells the history of clowns from the days of Pharoah to Marcel Marceau in only 50 pages.

SKILLS

Burgess, Hovey. **Circus Techniques.** Thomas Y. Crowell, New York, 1977.
Mr. Burgess is Master Teacher of Circus at New York University, and this is a masterly teaching book, with a series of carefully structured and illustrated lessons, delivered with confidence and a sprinkling of humorous and perceptive asides. Later editions carry a very useful appendix on Props, Rigging, Supplies and Sources (in the U.S.A.).

Carlo. **The Juggling Book.** Vintage Books, New York, 1974.
A book with a real "West Coast" feeling about it, although the author is from Baltimore and for a time ran his own "Circus Minimus" in New York City. His book takes a long time to explain not very much, but will be useful to you if you find my own Juggling chapter too brief. Carlo covers techniques of working with one to five balls and clubs, both individually and with a partner.

Wiley, Jack. **The Unicycle Book.** Stackpole Books, Harrisburg, PA, 1973.
Jack Wiley, who has also written on Acrobatics, Tumbling and Basic Circus Skills, is a real ENTHUSIAST. He has been building and riding unicycles since 7th grade. In this book he teaches how to build the things, and how to ride them, how to race with them, how to entertain with them. Illustrated.

ORGANIZATIONS AND MAGAZINES

Circus Fans Asoociation of America. Magazine, "White Tops," ed. by Melvin J. Olsen, 4931 Rosslyn, Indianapolis, IN 46205.

Circus Fans Association of Great Britain. Magazine, "King Pole," ed. by David Jamieson, 53 Park Court, Harrow, Essex, England.

International Jugglers Association, P.O. Box 443, Davidson, NC 28036.

Unicycle Society of America, c/o Joyce Jones, P.O. Box 40534, Redford, MI 48240.

Suitcase Circus Project, c/o Reg Bolton, 4 Stratford Road, Salisbury, Wiltshire, England.